Through the Eyes of Mark

Through the Eyes of Mark

His World, His Gospel

JACK CIANCIO

WIPF & STOCK · Eugene, Oregon

THROUGH THE EYES OF MARK
His World, His Gospel

Wipf & Stock
An Imprint of Wipf and Stock Publishers
199 W. 8th Ave., Suite 3
Eugene, OR 97401

www.wipfandstock.com

PAPERBACK ISBN: 978-1-6667-0796-0
HARDCOVER ISBN: 978-1-6667-0797-7
EBOOK ISBN: 978-1-6667-0798-4

07/19/21

As a gospel specialist, I tell my students that they need to perform a reader identification with the original readers in order to study the significance of a story for our day.

—GRANT OSBORNE, *THE HERMENEUTICAL SPIRAL*

Contents

Abbreviations

Acts	*Acts of the Apostles*
AH	Against Heresies
Ann	*Annals*
Ant.	Josephus, *Antiquities*
BCE	Before the Common Era or Before the Christian Era
ca	circa
CE	Common Era or Christian Era
Col	Colossians
Cor	Corinthians
Dan	Daniel
EH	*Ecclesiastical History*
fn	footnote
Gal	Galatians
Heb	Hebrews
J.W.	Josephus *War of the Jews* or *History of the Destruction of Jerusalem*
KJV	King James Version
LXX	Septuagint
Macc	Maccabees
NETS	A New English Translation of the Septuagint
NIV	New International Version
NRSV	New Revised Standard Version

NT	New Testament
OT	Old Testament
v	verse
vv	verses

Introduction

THE GOSPEL ACCORDING TO Mark is arguably the most compelling and yet bewildering, rewarding and yet frustrating, forthright and yet mystifying account of the life and ministry of Jesus Christ. It has been described as boring, plain, and artless, as well as being emotionally intense, realistic, and vivid. This diversity in descriptions makes for one very intriguing piece of literature. Beyond the coincidence that my birthday, April 25, falls on Mark's feast day, I never had any particular opinion one way or another about this Gospel. Except for its brevity[1] it didn't seem to be much different from any of the other gospels, basically offering the same parables, pericopes, and teachings about the life and ministry of Jesus Christ. A few years ago, however, that all changed—I discovered Mark.

While doing some academic research on the Synoptic Gospels (Mark, Luke, Matthew), I discovered in Mark a unique and multifaceted story, a narrative that hides a fascinating complexity behind a superficial simplicity. In Mark I found a canonical gospel that, on careful scrutiny, is out-of-line with the other Gospels. For example, in Mark, unlike the other three Gospels, the twelve apostles come across as befuddled. They never quite understand what Jesus is all about. In the end they abandon him as he suffers and dies alone. Why would Mark present the apostles, especially Peter, considered closest to Jesus and for whom Mark was the alleged translator, in such a disparaging manner? What did Mark know that the other Gospel writers did not? And why did subsequent editors of his Gospel find the ending of his original manuscript so troubling that they thought it necessary to add an ending of their own?

These and many other questions prompted me to delve into as many books and articles on Mark as I could find. The more I explored Mark's

---

1. It is shortest in *total* length compared to Matthew and Luke. If, however, one compares the length of shared pericopes, Mark's are most often longer (Stein, *Studying,* 53).

Gospel the more I found myself being pulled into a vortex of fascination. As if reading a slowly developing mystery novel my intrigue grew until I reached a point of appreciation that is best described by Morton Enslin: "The longer I study this gospel, the more I am impressed by the daring genius of its author. Far from being an artless work, it bears on every page the evidence . . . of the author's creative design."[2] Mark offers controversy, theological challenges, and fascinating insights into a world far removed, a world where myth intertwined with reality. His Gospel is not only a story about Jesus but also about the early church and the forces that influenced his telling of that story. Most people have heard selected scriptural verses from this Gospel hundreds of times in many worship services, and yet few realize the conflict and turmoil Mark was conveying in the words he used and in the words he purposefully avoided using. Without Mark it is possible that we would not have the Gospels of Matthew, Luke, or John and, therefore, no organized first-century written account of the ministry of Jesus. It is quite conceivable that without Mark's Gospel Christianity as we know it would never have come to fruition. If so, the history of Western Civilization would have been quite different.

If, as I have noted, there are so many books and articles on Mark's Gospel, you might ask, "Why *another*?" While there are numerous books and articles on this particular gospel, many of them are quite academic, written by and for scholars and theologians. Or they "preach" Mark rather than strive for an understanding of Mark. This book is different in that it offers the reader passage into Mark's world, to see that world through Mark's eyes and thus come to an understanding of what influenced Mark to write that particular Gospel in that particular form at that particular time in history. I have gathered the leadings of many scholars, theologians, and church historians hoping to give the reader a detailed look at Mark's world, his intention for writing the Gospel, what influenced him, the opposition and conflicts with which he struggled, and how that all culminated in a theology he hoped to convey to the burgeoning Christian church. In short, I wanted to get behind the eyes of the Evangelist to see the world as he saw it.

The difficulty in preparing a book on Mark and his Gospel is that we have an excess of suppositions about him, his Gospel, Jesus, and those formative years of the church, but very few definitive and verifiable facts. Sam Williams uses the term "informed conjecture" to define the process scholars have used to come up with the very best conclusions given so few verifiable facts.[3] Albert C. Outler cautions us that these are "ingenious conjectures as

---

2. Enslin, *The Artistry of Mark*, 388.
3. Williams, *Jesus' Death*, 205.

to how things 'really were.'"[4] William Wrede calls it "suppositionitis," historical guesswork at best.[5] All these suppositions are drawn from tidbits of historical information gleaned from various period writings such as the books of the New Testament, Apocryphal Books, Roman historical records, and the writings of the early church fathers. It helps that interwoven throughout those records are many verifiable historical facts that lead to well-reasoned conclusions. Nevertheless, the truth is that much of what we accept as fact is really drawn from specious suppositions. The human mind, perhaps more so 2,000 years ago than today, has a habit of allowing the imagination to fill in where facts run out. A more scientific way of stating that is to be found in the explanation for mental schemas.

A *schema* is a fixed mental representation either of how things are, or how we think they are or should be. It is formed by a combination of experience and learning.[6] Schemas are not a process of which the individual is consciously aware.[7] Through repeated exposure to similar stimuli, for example, experiences, teachings, and observations the individual subconsciously builds a cognitive model, a sort of mental data bank, that informs what to expect, what it means, how best to respond, the implications of, stereotypes, and a general repertoire of theories regarding new types of stimuli.[8] That pre-existing model then strongly influences the individual's response to new stimuli. The Gospel of John offers an excellent example of the schema challenge that Jesus as Messiah posed for the Jews. In John 12:32 Jesus says, "And I, when I am lifted up from the earth, will draw all people to myself." This, however, was counter to the schematic representation of the Messiah affixed in the minds of the Jews. John exposes this cognitive conflict in 12:34, "The crowd answered him, 'We have heard from the law that the Messiah remains forever. How can you say that the Son of Man will be lifted up?'" Centuries of authoritative teaching had formed a schema of the Messiah in the minds of the Jews that was dramatically different from that described by Jesus.[9] Schemas work syllogistically from the information that has been laid down from prior experience. Such prior experience

---

4. Outler, "The Gospel," 4.

5. Wrede, *The Messianic Secret*, 8.

6. Beck and Clark. "Anxiety and Depression", 24.

7. Rest, *Postconventional Moral Thinking*, 136.

8. Narvaez and Bock, *Moral Schema*, 300.

9 This example is of particular importance throughout this study for two reasons: 1) It is a perfect example of the inflexibility of a schema; 2) it well explains the conflict between early Christianity and Judaism as it exemplifies the conflict between the traditional Jewish schema of the Messiah and the dramatically new and conflicting Christian proclamation of the suffering-servant messiahship of Jesus.

then influences new decision-making.[10] If, therefore, a person's experience or instruction has always been "If *A* then *B*," then any situation that presents pre-existing schemata *A* (for example, the Messiah will remain forever) will facilitate the assumption that *B* follows (therefore, the Messiah cannot be "lifted up"). Trying to reconcile "what I know" with information that shows "what I know might be wrong" creates what modern psychology calls *cognitive dissonance,* an incompatibility of beliefs, which leads to a negative emotional state as the individual tries to resolve the issue.[11] Little wonder the Jews had difficulty accepting as the long-awaited Messiah this poor suffering peasant who was eventually condemned and executed as a common rebel. They were assured their Messiah would come in glory to vanquish Israel's foes and remain with them forever.

Schemas play another crucial function, which is that they help fill in gaps of missing information.[12] Where no knowledge exists to verify the facts and render a certifiable response the mind will configure a "close enough" response based on knowledge already encoded. This explains why many of the suppositional particulars of those early church years have come to be accepted as fact when, in reality, there is no credible evidence to support their validity. For example, it is widely assumed that the "John whose other name was Mark" (Acts 12:12) was the author of the Gospel according to Mark but there are no facts to support such a claim. Our need to fill in this gap is accommodated by our subconscious schema processing rendering us more comfortable with some answer that fills in a missing piece of the puzzle rather than no answer. In the Acts of the Apostles we have a historical figure named John Mark, sometimes called Mark, a name that appears several times but with no other reference as to identity, and we have a Gospel that tradition has titled "Mark"; therefore, because they have in common certain schematic facts—place, historical time, associates, group affiliation—it must be the same Mark. And yet, there is no proof John Mark or, as will be shown, an individual named Mark, was the author of this Gospel.

Contributing to the difficulty of coming to a full understanding of Mark is that, while it is true that there is a lot of material written about the Gospel of Mark, much of it is inconsistent and contradictory. This led to what I found to be the "candy shop" effect—so many good suppositional "facts" to choose from that choosing one fact over another was difficult. In the end it came down to drawing conclusions from the preponderance of

10. Lipson, "The Influence," 449.

11. Harmon-Jones, "A Cognitive Dissonance Theory," 185, 192.

12 Lipson, "The Influence," 449; Rest, *Postconventional Moral Thinking,* 136.

information and what formed the most logical conclusion based on available facts rather than on theological suppositions.

This book is limited to a compilation of what years of research by numerous scholars has determined to be the factors that influenced Mark, the unique genre Mark created with his Gospel, and the message that he was attempting to convey to the rest of the first-century Christian community. There will be differing opinions (informed conjectures), to be sure, but generating differing opinions is one of the most alluring characteristics of Mark and his Gospel. This is not an evangelical lecture on what to believe nor does it offer a theological position. Through this analytical deconstruction of the Gospel according to Mark readers will gain insights into Mark's world, the historical events, and the worldview of first-century citizens that shaped his writing. In brief, I invite readers to set aside their schematic beliefs and to look behind the scenes to see what Mark saw and experienced in his world that led him to write that particular narrative, at that particular time, and in that particular format.

PART I

Conflict and Betrayal

1

Mark and His World

WHAT WOULD EVENTUALLY BECOME the Gospel according to Mark essentially began immediately following the death of Jesus. Although we theorize about a much later date of creation, the truth is that all the forces that eventually shaped Mark's final product began with the realization that Jesus was gone and his followers were on their own, a disorganized group of believers in—what? Even they were unsure about how or why their beloved Jesus ended up crucified as a rebel. Despite the confusion and doubts and within a cauldron of political, religious, and cultural events the memory of Jesus was kept vibrantly alive in the hearts and minds of his followers. It is within that cauldron that we must look for those seminal events that would lead to the creation of the Gospel according to Mark.

To fully understand this Gospel we must know the world in which Mark lived and how he perceived it. With that in mind we must first engage in what is known as redaction criticism, which is the investigation of the Gospel traditions, so that we may better understand the life situation of the Evangelists that led them to write their Gospels. In New Testament studies, the German term *Sitz im Leben* (situation in life), refers to the circumstances, conditions, the happenings that we, two thousand years removed, in a different culture, language, and knowledge of the world, and a wholly different religious schema, deduce as influencing those to whom we attribute the creation of the four Gospels. We are interested in the *Sitz im Leben* of the Evangelist himself when he "wrote" his gospel. Here we must pause to ask, "Did the Evangelists really *write* their Gospels?" Not in the sense

3

that Dickens wrote his novels. The Gospels are a collection of oral stories told, bits of written information, and sermons preached over the years from the crucifixion to the first formal written gospel narrative. The redactors, that is, editors, of the Gospels compiled those narratives by selecting and organizing what information already existed about Jesus within the growing Christian community. Along with what they selected they added their own material to both improve the flow of their narratives and to advance their own personal theological opinion.[1] The resultant Gospels were strongly influenced by the *Sitz im Leben* of each individual Evangelist and the needs of the Christian community.

To better understand Mark we need to know the religious, political, and cultural forces that affected his thinking, beliefs, and goals. How did the early believers receive and understand Mark? As will be shown, first-century Christians did not trust the written word, so we must wonder how Mark hoped to get his message of the "Good News" across not only in written form but in a form never before seen. To understand Mark's Gospel, we really need to know his world. As much as possible, we must try to understand that world by recognizing that first-century cognitive processes, that is, how the brain processes information, would not yield the same results as our twenty-first-century cognitive processes. Mark wrote in *Koine* Greek,[2] the Greek of the first century, which is not the same as modern-day Greek. The words in Mark's text do not function for us today as they did for his first-century audience, whether Christian or Gentile. We must immerse ourselves in Greek philosophy and literature, Roman paganism and power, Judaic literature and theology, and the traditional myths of all those cultures to understand Mark and this burgeoning movement of "believers" not yet known as Christians. What was going on in the community of believers, the Jewish nation, and the pagan Roman Empire that prompted Mark to write? And why did he choose this never-before-seen form in which to write? Most importantly, how do the answers to those questions affect our faith today?

Mark Who?

Who wrote the Gospel according to Mark? Traditional theory claims that the author of this Gospel is the "John whose other name was Mark," mentioned in Acts 12:12.[3] It is accepted that this Mark accompanied Paul and Barnabas on

---

1. Dodd, *The Founder*, 26.

2. The form of Greek, mostly derived from the Attic dialect, that became the standard language for Greek-speaking people during the Hellenistic period.

3. Lea and Black, *The New Testament*, 141.

their missionary journeys to Seleucia, Cyprus, Salamis, Paphos, and Perga. It was in Perga, for some undisclosed reason, that Mark left them to return to Jerusalem (Acts13:4–13). Later, when Paul asked Barnabas to set out on another missionary journey, Barnabas wanted to take Mark, but Paul refused, citing Mark's "desertion" of them at Pamphylia. This did not sit well with Barnabas and he left Paul and set out with Mark for Cyprus (Acts 15:36–39). While we will never know what caused the rift we do read that it was "sharp" (Acts 15:39). It seems quite likely that, from John Mark's perspective, being accused of desertion was not something to be taken lightly. This raises important questions. Was Paul's rejection based on theological differences? Missionary techniques? If John Mark was the author of this Gospel how might these differences and Paul's sharp rejection of having him along influence Mark's subsequent narrative?

Other references to Mark include Colossians 4:10, which mentions greetings being sent by "Mark the cousin of Barnabas." While none of these references provide evidence that John Mark wrote the Gospel, they do indicate that there was a "Mark," an individual who was significantly involved with the initial organization of the Christian church, someone who was intimately acquainted with the thoughts, actions, and goals of the most influential founders of the church itself. There is little doubt that this Mark, John or otherwise, was qualified to produce a narrative of the earthly ministry of Jesus.

There is more in the traditional theory that suggests that Mark was the author of the Gospel and that this Mark served as Peter's interpreter in Rome, translating Peter's Aramaic into Greek. The original Christian historian Eusebius Pamphilus (ca. 260 to ca. 340 CE) writing in his *Ecclesiastical History* (ca. 325 CE) makes two references to Mark and this Gospel. This first reference follows mention of Peter's martyrdom.

> So greatly, however, did the splendor of piety enlighten the minds of Peter's hearers, that it was not sufficient to hear but once, nor to receive the unwritten doctrine of the gospel of God, but they persevered in every variety of entreaties, to solicit Mark as a companion of Peter, and whose gospel we have, that he should leave them a monument of the doctrine thus orally communicated in writing. Nor did they cease their solicitations until they had prevailed with the man, and thus become the means of that history which is called the Gospel according to Mark (2:15).[4]

---

4. All references to Eusebius's *Ecclesiastical History* (*EH*) are from the Cruse translation.

Elsewhere in *Ecclesiastical History*, Eusebius quotes a letter written some-time between 95 and 120 CE from Papias (ca.70 to 163 CE), Bishop of Hierapolis, who attests to "a tradition" claiming Mark was the author of the Gospel, then adds:

> And John the Presbyter also said this, "Mark being the inter-preter of Peter, whatsoever he recorded he wrote with great ac-curacy but not however, in the order in which it was spoken or done by our Lord, for he neither heard nor followed our Lord, but as before said, he was in company with Peter, who gave him such instructions as was necessary, but not to give a history of our Lord's discourses; wherefore Mark has not erred in any-thing, by writing some things as he has recorded them; for he was carefully attentive to one thing, not to pass by anything that he heard, or to state anything falsely in these accounts" (3:39).

The church father Irenaeus (ca. 125 to 202 CE), writing early in the second century, supports this theory: "After their [the disciples'] departure Mark, the disciple and interpreter of Peter, did also hand down to us in writing what had been preached by Peter."[5]

Regrettably, none of these three sources offer any direct evidence that John Mark wrote this Gospel. The fact is the titled author is an assumed name. Because the Gospel has been given the name of "Mark," we assume it was written by one person. In all likelihood there was more than one person involved in putting out the final product. Harold Guy contends that each Gospel is the work of a preacher, a compiler, and an editor.[6] The preacher had in his possession several oral stories regarding Jesus that he had collected and preached over the years and eventually transcribed to papyrus sheets. The compiler collected the individual sheets and the redactor (editor), who had other Jesus material, sought to create a comprehensive story by combining other material with that of the compiler, thus giving birth to what we now know as the Gospel according to Mark. Enslin opines that Mark took a much more active, artistic, and purposeful role in creating his narrative.[7] Chronol-ogy was not as important as the total portrait, confirming what Papias said "not to give a history of our Lord's discourses; wherefore Mark has not erred in anything, by writing some things as he has recorded them."

We do know from all that has been stated above that there was a very prominent person named Mark involved in the early church. Evidence

---

5. Irenaeus, *Against Heresies*, (3.1.1).

6. Guy, *The Origin*, 141. Dodd, *The Founder*, 24, considers Mark more the compiler than the writer.

7. Enslin, "The Artistry," 388.

confirming the traditional author as John Mark cannot, however, be verified, especially since Mark (Μάρκο or Marcus), was a popular Greco-Roman name at that time.[8] As was the tradition of the times, author names were attached to these documents for various reasons, perhaps chosen because the name was well known or held more authority for the intended audience. Since John Mark was a well-known associate of the apostles and well connected within the early church, the final work may have been issued under his name.[9] Contributing to the elusiveness of an exact identification of the author is the fact that all four Gospels were in circulation for many years before any name was attached to them.[10] We must admit, no matter how reluctantly, that claiming John Mark as the author of this Gospel is one of those schema-filling psychological processes mentioned earlier. In truth, the true identity of the author of the Gospel according to Mark is lost to us.[11]

The author's true identity, however, is not the focus of this study, which is to examine the author's world as it influenced him to write his narrative of Jesus. As Grant Osborne explains, "We don't study the author but the author's intended message. There we see those concerns, values and theological perspectives that the original author has chosen to highlight in this particular text."[12] For the sake of clarity and consistency throughout this examination we will accept from tradition that someone named Mark, possibly an associate of Peter, wrote this Gospel in or near Rome.[13] What motivated him to write and his goals for writing as well as the accepted fact that it was the first Gospel written are topics waiting to be discussed. This Mark probably did not know the historical Jesus (as stated by Eusebius), but could well have been intimately associated with the post-crucifixion Christian community, perhaps Jesus' apostles in general, and Peter in particular. There are some who speculate that this Mark was also the young man who ran away naked after losing his "linen cloth" following a scuffle with those who arrested Jesus at Gethsemane (Mark 14:51–52).[14] Mark's is the only Gospel in which this incident is mentioned and there is no evidence to support that conclusion. Indeed, it will be shown later that perhaps such

8. Kok, "The Flawed Evangelist," 244.

9. Guy, *The Origin*, 144.

10. Ehrman, *How Jesus*, 90.

11. Enslin, "The Artistry," 387.

12. Osborne, *The Hermeneutical Spiral*, 204.

13. There is no definitive proof that Mark's Gospel was written in Rome (Marxsen, *Mark the Evangelist*, 23, fn 26). Mark's is the only Gospel associated with a city.

14. Lea and Black, *The New Testament*, 141.

an incident never occurred but was a literary device used by the Gospel's author to convey a metaphysical point.

Authorship notwithstanding, questions of profound importance beg answering; most importantly, "Why was this Gospel written at all?"[15] Why, indeed? What prompted Mark to write this narrative when he did? Was he writing an *apologia*, that is, an explanatory defense, of the work and ministry of Jesus and the work of the church, or was he defending a certain theological position he preferred against what he saw as an errant interpretation of Jesus' ministry? Did he want to correct the course of a movement that he saw as deviating from the course Jesus intended, or did he just want to synthesize all the random oral and written tidbits about Jesus that were being exchanged among the believers within the community of this burgeoning faith? Or, did he feel a sense of foreboding, an impending doom, and want to record the facts as he understood them before—what?

Time of Writing

It is impossible to establish an exact date for the composition of Mark's Gospel. Indeed, the dating of the Gospel has historically been a contested academic issue. When we talk about a date of composition we should consider that it may have been a year or two in the making, or that it may have been written and put aside for some time before it was released to the rest of the Christian community. We simply do not know. Later, as we examine the historical setting and events, as well as the content of Mark's narrative of Jesus' ministry, we will find clues that allow us to hone in on the most likely date of composition.

The best that can be hoped for is a *time period*, and even here scholars vary in their estimation with dates ranging from sometime in the 40s CE to 71 CE. Given the intervening two thousand years, this slight time difference seems insignificant. Choosing an earlier or later date, however, affects our knowledge not only of what influenced Mark's writing but also the message he was trying to convey and, therefore, our understanding of the Gospel. Each of those time periods saw specific historical events that affected the growing Christian church. Table 1 below will help put into perspective significant historic events that would affect Mark's *Sitz im Leben*.

---

15. Cadbury, "Gospel Study," 139; Guy, *The Origin*, 14.

Year	Event
33	The approximate year of the execution of Jesus.
33–60s	Ongoing rift between the Jewish Christians (Judaizers/Jerusalem church) led by James, and the Hellenistic Christians led by Stephen and Paul.
35–38?	Stephen martyred and Hellenists spread teaching throughout Middle East—Alexandria, Rome, Syria. (Date is difficult to determine with any degree of certainty.)
42	Peter escapes after being imprisoned by Herod Agrippa. On the run as a wanted fugitive, his evasion may have taken him to Alexandria and to Rome.
49	Emperor Claudius expels Jews from Rome.
49	Jerusalem Council convened with Peter and Paul present.
57	Paul pens his Epistle to the Romans.
60–62	Paul arrives in Rome to stand trial.
64	Burning of Rome.
65	Neronian persecutions of Christians begins.
66	First Roman-Jewish War begins.
65–69	Execution of Peter and Paul either during Neronian persecution or Roman-Jewish War.
70	Roman-Jewish War ends with the destruction of Jerusalem and the Temple; Diaspora of Christian and non-Christian Jews from Jerusalem; end of the Christian Jerusalem church.
71	Titus' triumphal parade in Rome displaying spoils from the conquest of Judea, including remnants from the Temple.

Table 1: Significant historic events

If Mark compiled this Gospel in the late 50s to early 60s CE then he would have been writing to a growing community of believers that, while trying to make sense of just who this Jesus was, the message he brought, and their role in carrying on his ministry, was also being pulled in two different directions—one Jewish, the other Hellenistic. If he wrote in the middle to late 60s, then he would have been influenced by a disorganized church tormented by the Neronian persecution and the martyrdom of its two prominent leaders, Paul and Peter. If his Gospel was written after 70 CE, then all those conditions above apply, to which we must add the facts that he was writing after the Roman-Jewish War, the fall of Jerusalem, the destruction of the Second Temple, the subsequent Diaspora from Jerusalem of not only the orthodox Jews but also those Jews who were known as *believers*, soon-to-be Christians, and the end of the Jerusalem church. In that event, Mark would have seen his faith-movement on the brink of elimination. He would have seen that first generation, the era of the apostles, coming to an end and with that end the last remaining link between the historical Jesus and the world. Perhaps that was his motivation for putting his Gospel together. To understand Mark's world we must go back to where it started.

Believers Beset By Conflict

Our general schema of the development of Christianity is that it was linear, that is, a direct development from the crucifixion to final adoption as the official religion of the Roman Empire. In fact, it was anything but. The crucifixion was followed by years of dissimilar splinter groups claiming to be followers of Jesus. In short, Christianity grew out of various but distinctly Jewish sects. Initially, it would have been quite difficult to distinguish between Jewish Christians (Judaizers) and Orthodox Jews. This new sect, which would not even be known as "Christian" for quite some time (Acts 11:26), was still dedicated to its ancestral religion. It was Jewish in form, manner, thought, and identity.[16] Both groups attended the same temple (Acts 2:46) and prayed the same prayers (Acts 2:42). Jewish Christians, some of whom were so rooted in Judaism that they are identified in Acts 15:5 as belonging to "the sect of the Pharisees," conformed to and upheld all the conditions of Judaism—circumcision, adherence to the Torah, observance of traditional Jewish feast days, maintenance of dietary (kosher) restrictions, etc. They believed that a risen Jesus was the fulfillment of the messianic promise to Israel and soon God's Spirit would descend upon them.[17] Jewish Christians also staunchly held to the belief that to be a member of this new sect one still had to meet and maintain those qualifying markers of being a Jew, that is, circumcision, the Law (Torah), dietary restrictions, etc. (Acts 15:5).

Christianity might have been sired by Judaism but it grew on the mother's milk of Greek culture.[18] During those embryonic years of the church in Jerusalem there existed two different Jewish cultures. Those that accepted Jesus as Messiah but otherwise held strictly to traditional Jewish religious tradition are referred to as "Hebrew" in Acts 6:1. The other, known as "Hellenist," consisted of Greek-speaking ethnic Jews. The Hellenistic culture was deeply embedded in first-century Palestine. Its roots extended back nearly 300 years to the successful invasion by Alexander the Great and the subsequent division of the Middle East into Greek-ruled territories. In

---

16. Walls, "Converts or Proselytes?" 4.

17. Kraus, "The Early Church," 259.

18. McKechnie, *The First Christian Centuries*, 12.

the year 167 BCE Antiochus IV Epiphanes of Syria, a descendant of that Greek line of rulers, tried to forcefully impose Hellenistic culture and rule on the Jews by banning their Law and sacred books, and attempting to convert the Temple to pagan worship.[19] This gave rise to the Maccabean revolt, which will be discussed in more detail in chapter 5. Although the Hellenistic culture—its literature, philosophy, language, and religious worldview—was deeply assimilated into Jewish life, historic evidence points to a long-standing antagonism between the two cultures. The Hellenists abandoned many of their Jewish traditions, including religion, and incorporated many aspects of Greek culture and philosophy into their lives. Jerusalem went so far as to create a Greek constitution, making Greek citizenship available to its citizens.[20] This separation within the Jewish culture led to an increasing use of the Greek language and decreasing use of Hebrew, so much so that a need arose to translate the Hebrew Bible into Greek, resulting in the Septuagint Bible (LXX), which became the main resource for the first Christian authors.[21] The entire Jewish culture, including Jesus, would have been subjected to Hellenism. The assimilation of the Greek worldview into Jewish culture dramatically affected not only the primitive church's interpretation of Jesus as Christ but also Christianity's subsequent theological development. Two of the most profound influences on the development of Christian thought were the philosophies of Plato and the Greek Stoics.[22]

The Jewish Christians were led by a de facto authority of James, the brother of Jesus, Peter, and John,[23] and perhaps other original apostles. It was centered in Jerusalem, regularly worshipped in the Temple, and is commonly referred to as the Jerusalem Church, Palestinian church, or Jewish Christianity. Its authority, philosophy, and theology, however, were challenged by the Hellenistic Christians, most prominently Stephen, Philip, and, eventually, Paul. This Hellenist sect was a movement breaking away from Judaic orthodox tradition. The Acts of the Apostles, chapters 6 and 7 in particular, clearly reveals this conflict. These differences created a power struggle and growing antagonism that eventually led to outright hostility between the two factions. An example can be found in Acts 6:1 where it is

19. Josephus, *Antiquities*, 12: Ch. 1–5.

20. Kraus, "The Early Church," 252.

21. Gonzàlez, *A History*, 40–2.

22. Gonzàlez, *A History*, 50–3. As an example, the concept of the *Logos* of John 1:1 was initially put forth nearly 500 years earlier by the pre-Socratic philosopher Heraclitus (Reynolds, *When Athens*, 39). The Logos was a main aspect of Stoicism, a prominent Greek philosophical belief system that greatly influenced the development of Christianity (Gonzàlez, *A History*, 52–3).

23. Paul refers to these three as the "acknowledged pillars" of the church (Gal 2–9).

noted that a complaint was brought by the Hellenists against "the Hebrews" over the distribution of food, which would have been an issue of serious consequence if it occurred during the famine in the 40s CE. At stake was the future nature of Christianity because whoever assumed authority would determine the future of the faith. James, by nature of his relationship to Jesus, and Peter and John as apostles who lived at Jesus' side throughout his earthly ministry and were privy not only to his public but also his private teachings (Mark 4:10), assumed they had the authority to lead. Their intimate connection to the Lord certainly gave them the credentials to do so. God sent Jesus to them, and Jesus sent them to the world. To their way of thinking there was a direct line running from God, through Jesus, through them to the world. Their authority seemed self-evident.

Paul, on the other hand, was a late comer, a self-appointed apostle, claiming that right because of his mystical confrontation with the Lord on the road to Damascus (Acts 9:27). Paul posed a significant and continuing challenge to James and the others. Acts is replete with examples of their ongoing conflict. The Acts of the Apostles was written by Luke,[24] a traveling companion of Paul (Col 4:14) and seems to be heavily biased in Paul's favor. Acts begins with the spotlight on Peter but ends with it on Paul who generally dominates the latter half of the book. In Acts, Luke suggests no apostolic distinction between Paul and the chosen Twelve. This bias may have influenced what Luke put in and left out of Acts. It is interesting to note that in all of Paul's extant writings, which were written long before Luke's Acts, he never gives us the specific details of the event on the road to Damascus as Luke does in Acts 9.

As Christianity grew in numbers, it also grew as a threat to the established orthodox Jewish establishment. Acts 6:11–14 reflects growing anti-Christian sentiment when Stephen, a Hellenist, is accused by "some of those who belonged to the synagogue" for teaching contrary to "Moses and God" (Acts 6:9–11). This led to Stephen's execution followed by a scattering of "all except for the apostles" (Acts 8:1). If the original apostles were exempted, then the "all" must refer specifically to the Hellenists. As a result the Hellenists became the leading missionaries to a large region beyond Judea, that is, Samaria (Acts 8:5), Caesarea (Acts 8:40), Phoenicia, Cyprus, and Antioch (Acts 11:19). Paul, himself, indicates that his Hellenist missionary work was more prevalent outside of Judea: "Then I went to the regions of Syria and Cilicia[25] and I was still unknown by sight to the churches of Judea that are

24. "Luke" is a pseudonym. As in the case of Mark, we do not know the exact author of Luke/Acts. Whoever it was most certainly wrote the Gospel that bears the name.

25 An area of Asia Minor including modern-day southeastern Turkey and Cyprus.

in Christ . . . " (Gal 1:21–22). The Jewish Christians followed behind the Hellenist missionaries in spreading the faith beyond Judea.[26]

It is obvious that there was great diversity in thought leading to conflict within the primitive church. Paul gives us a glimpse of conflict within the expanding church when he writes, "For to begin with, when you come together as a church, I hear that there are divisions among you; and to some extent I believe it" (1 Cor 11:18). According to Acts 9:22, Paul was "becoming increasingly more powerful and confounded the Jews who lived in Damascus by proving that Jesus was the Messiah." Shortly thereafter, however, when he tried to join the disciples in Jerusalem he was rejected because they were afraid of him (v. 26). The actual explosive point between the Jerusalem church and the Hellenists, however, was brought on by Paul's aggressive missionary activity among the Gentiles,[27] often referred to as "Greeks,"[28] who were ethnically non-Jews. The contentious point was how much of orthodox Judaism did the Gentiles have to abide by to be included within the group of believers. Did they have to be circumcised? Observe the feasts? Maintain Jewish dietary restrictions? Adhere to Torah? The Pharisaic sect of the Jerusalem church was resolute in insisting they did, whereas Paul was just as resolute in saying no, they did not. More than just *no,* Paul said the Jerusalem church was altogether missing the point of Jesus' message and ministry. For the Jerusalem church, observance of the Law was necessary not only for moral integrity but also for maintaining a righteous nation before God. Jewish Israel's dedication to the Torah and monotheism distinguished it from all other religions, nations, and ethnicities. Paul saw Jesus' ministry as having made the Law obsolete and in its place we have the Holy Spirit and the new Scripture (Heb 8:6–7) to provide righteous guidance. The two sides also disagreed on the indwelling of God's kingdom. The Jerusalem church believed that it was already here, whereas Paul taught that it was a future event.[29] Essentially, two opposing groups of Christians emerged: the Jewish Christians (Jerusalem or Palestinian church) led by the original apostles, and the Hellenists, led by Stephen, Philip, and Paul. There were marked oppositional differences between these two groups.[30]

As regards convincing others on the conditions to be placed on Gentiles, Acts 15:5 notes, "But some believers who belonged to the sect of the Pharisees stood up and said, 'It is necessary for them [Gentile converts]

26. Cullmann, "Dissension Within," 86.
27. Kraus, "The Early Church," 263.
28. Walls, "Converts or Proselytes?" 4.
29. DeBoer, "Saint Paul Versus," 165.
30. Gonzàlez, *A History,* 40; DeBoer, "Saint Paul Versus," 164.

to be circumcised and ordered to keep the law of Moses.'" To refer to this group of believers as "Pharisees" indicates how serious the growth of this new "sect" as part of the established orthodox Jewish religion, accepted even by some priests (Acts 6:7), had become. But Paul and the Hellenist faction saw Jesus' messiahship as signalling a break from the old covenant (Heb 8:6–7) and the Law. In this new covenant the Gentiles are to be included: "There is no longer Jew or Greek" (Gal 3:28); " . . . there is no longer Greek and Jew, circumcised and uncircumcised . . . " (Col 3:11), without having to qualify as Jews by adhering to traditional Jewish orthodoxy.

Acts 15:6–35 informs us that in a general council held in Jerusalem (ca. 49 CE) the leaders of the Jerusalem church and Paul came to an agreement. It was decided that Gentiles can be counted among the believers and saved without being circumcised as long as they "abstain from what has been sacrificed to idols and from blood and from what has been strangled and from fornication" (v. 29). As to who was best capable and should minister to the Gentiles, Acts 15:6–7 tells us, "The apostles and the elders met together to consider this matter. After there had been much debate, Peter stood up and said to them, 'My brothers, you know that in the early days God made a choice among you, that I should be the one through whom the Gentiles would hear the message of the good news and become believers.'" Paul, however, viewed matters quite differently when he wrote to the Galatians:

> But when Cephas [Peter] came to Antioch, I opposed him to his face, because he stood self-condemned. For until certain people came from James, he used to eat with the Gentiles. After they came he drew back and kept himself separate for fear of the circumcision faction. The other Jews joined him in this hypocrisy, so that even Barnabas was led astray by their hypocrisy. When I saw that they were not acting consistently with the truth of the gospel, I said to Cephas before them all, if you, though a Jew, live like a Gentile and not like a Jew, how can you compel the Gentiles to live like Jews? (Gal 2:11–14).

The two factions eventually settled into recognizing Peter as missionary to the circumcised, and Paul as missionary to the uncircumcised (Gal 2:8).

The confrontation between Paul and the Palestinian church leaders detailed in Acts 21 support the fact that, although Paul's power was growing, James and the elders were still in charge. Some troubling reports about Paul's missionary work prompted James and the elders to impose a rite of purification upon Paul and necessitated some clarifying followup to those "Gentiles who have become believers, we have sent a letter with our judgment that they should abstain from what has been sacrificed to idols and from blood and from what is strangled and from fornication" (v 25), but no need to be circumcised.

Paul, in this instance, bowed to the authority of James and the others. But his resentment of the apostolic leadership is evident from what he later wrote to the Galatians:

> And from those who were supposed to be acknowledged leaders (what they actually were makes no difference to me; God shows no partiality)—those leaders contributed nothing to me. On the contrary, when they saw that I had been entrusted with the gospel for the uncircumcised, just as Peter had been entrusted with the gospel to the circumcised (for he who worked through Peter making him an apostle to the circumcised also worked through me and sending me to the Gentiles), and when James and Cephas and John, who were acknowledged pillars, recognized the grace that had been given me, they gave to Barnabas and me the right hand of fellowship, agreeing that we should go to the Gentiles and they to the circumcised(2:6–9).

Acts of the Apostles is not a chronologically accurate narrative of what occurred in those formative years after the death of Jesus. Its jumble of events does, however, reveal a new embryonic theology seeking a place for itself, one which was often persecuted for its threatening ambitions. It was a growing organization that was being challenged by an enthusiastic, ambitious outsider who once breathed "threats and murder against the disciples of the Lord" (Acts 9:1), some of whom now led the church. Acts makes abundantly clear that there was a definitive split and antagonism between the Hellenists led by Paul and the Jerusalem church, and between both of those groups and the orthodox Jewish establishment. It is impossible for us, two thousand years culturally, ethnically, and religiously removed, to grasp the emotional polarization and antagonisms that divided the Jews, the Jerusalem church, and the Hellenists but that division was decisive in the future development of Christianity.

Acts concludes with a mixed review of Paul's reception in Rome under arrest (ca. 62 CE). Acts 28:15 tells us that the believers came from near and far to greet him. The Jews in Rome, however, were not quite as receptive. Acts 28:17–28 tells us how Paul arranged a meeting with the local leaders who were curious because " . . . with regard to this sect [Christians] we know that everywhere it is spoken against" (v. 22). When he next met with the larger congregation some believed him, others did not. After insulting the non-believers, Paul tells them, "Let it be known to you then that this salvation of God has been sent to the Gentiles; they will listen" (v. 28). This alienation of the orthodox Jews from the Christian *sect*, would have grave implications later.

Acts 28:23–28 tells us that Paul encountered a mixed reception when he arrived in Rome, under arrest. The church in Rome was likely founded and maintained by those Hellenists who scattered after Stephen's martyrdom,[31] therefore they are most likely the ones who were accepting of Paul. How well received was Paul's theology by the members of the Jerusalem church there is unknown. Regardless, the conclusion of Acts suggests the growing importance of the church in Rome at the expense of the church in Jerusalem.[32] While this transfer of authority would not go unchallenged, historical events would soon make the transfer a *fait accompli* well beyond the control of either church faction.

Whoever this Mark was he would have been well aware of the conflicts between Paul and both the Jerusalem church and the orthodox Jews. If he was in Rome, his worldview would have been greatly influenced by events in that imperial city.

31. Snape, "Christian Origins," 231.
32. Snape, "Christian Origins," 234

2

Rome

Rome, where all things hideous and shameful from every part of the world find their centre and become popular.

—Tacitus, *Annals*

Although there is no definitive proof of exactly where Mark wrote his Gospel, tradition holds that it was written in or near Rome. Regardless of the exact location of his writing or how much time Mark spent in Rome, the political and religious state of affairs in the empire's capital city had a profound influence on his work. Our understanding of Mark, therefore, will be bolstered by examining the most influential persons and events in Mark's Roman world. These would include Peter, Paul, the Jews, the Roman church, and Imperial Rome—especially Roman attitudes and actions toward both Jews and Christians. The most significant events would be a city-wide inferno and a war of rebellion.

PETER AND PAUL

Peter

If we accept that Mark was Peter's interpreter, it follows that he was extensively familiar with Peter's theology, a theology aligned with the Jerusalem church. With that in mind we must then consider what influence Peter might have had on Mark's narrative, which requires us to learn more about Peter. Although we have come to accept Peter's central involvement with the founding of the Christian community after Jesus' death, he is, nevertheless, a rather enigmatic figure. Two traditional sources of Peter's work are Roman Catholic teachings and the Acts of the Apostles. Catholics contend (based not on Mark, his supposed interpreter, but on Matthew 16:18: "You are Peter, and on this rock I will build my church.") that Peter was given the mandate to sustain and grow Jesus' Kingdom on earth. The Gospels portray an exceptionally close relationship between Jesus and Peter. Catholic tradition also informs us that Peter was one of the founding authorities of the church in Rome, is recognized as its first Bishop, and, as such, was the first of the long dynasty of popes. Papal authority derives from this theory of apostolic succession.

None of the Gospels, the Acts of the Apostles, or the two letters written under Peter's name offer information as to the role Peter played in either the founding of or leadership in the church in Rome. There is, however, some supporting indirect evidence from other sources. The Acts of Peter, an Apocryphal book, offers anecdotal details regarding Peter's visits to and work in Rome. We read in that book that while Peter was still in Jerusalem he received a vision from the Lord to go to Rome to counter the heretical teachings of Simon Magus (5:3).[1] This is confirmed by Eusebius who mentions Peter going to Rome in pursuit of this heretic (*EH* 2.14). The author of 2 Peter may have had Simon Magus in mind when he warns of false teachers within the church (2:1). If Paul was referring to Peter in Romans 15:20–22 where he expresses his reluctance to go to Rome "so that I do not build on someone else's foundation"—who but Peter would have had such standing in the church to cause Paul to balk at crossing his path—then Peter would have been in Rome prior to 57 CE, the approximate date of Paul's letter.[2] It is also plausible that Peter did not go to Rome until such time as he was

---

1. *Magus* or *Magos*, a label that can be traced back to Plato, means "liar." (Liefeld, "The Helenistic 'Divine Man,'" 198).

2. Lea and Black, *The New Testament*, 391.

needed to shore up the morale of the Jewish Christians during the Neronian persecution.[3]

The Acts of the Apostles begins with Peter taking the leadership role in the Jerusalem church as one of the "pillars." Besides portraying him as the primary evangelist to the general crowds following the death of Jesus, Acts also tells us of his roving ministry: "Now as Peter went here and there among all the believers . . . " (Acts 9:32). In 42 CE he was imprisoned by order of Herod Agrippa. After his arrest and imprisonment his leadership role appears to decline, which makes sense considering that, having escaped imprisonment, he was on the lam as a wanted fugitive. His "wanted" status would not have been confined only to Judea but active throughout much of the eastern part of the Empire. Emperor Claudius had recently granted control of the region to Herod Agrippa, the same Agrippa who ordered the execution of James, brother of John (Acts 12:2–3). Josephus notes that, in addition to Judea, Agrippa, who reigned from 41–44 CE, was given administrative authority over Samaria and parts of the surrounding region as well (*Ant.* 19:5:1). Consequently, Agrippa's search for Peter covered a wide swath of territory that would have been wise for Peter to avoid. How passionate was Agrippa about recapturing Peter? Consider that when he learned Peter had escaped he "examined the guards and ordered them to be put to death" (Acts 12:19).

After escaping from prison, Peter immediately ran to the house of Mary, mother of John Mark (Acts 12:12), and while there he asked those already gathered in prayer to "tell James and the believers" of his escape. Since James, the brother of John, had been put to death, Peter must have meant James, the brother of Jesus. Such deference, even from Peter, is indication of James' importance as a leader of the Jerusalem church. Where did Peter go after leaving Mary's house? Did Mark go with him? There are indications that Alexandria, Egypt, was one of Peter's post-imprisonment destinations.[4] Alexandria was home to the largest Jewish community in the Greek-speaking world,[5] albeit much more Hellenized than the Palestinian Jewish community.[6] It would have been ripe for evangelization by a leader of the Jerusalem church and also large enough for a fugitive to safely blend in. Eusebius tells us that Mark was also active in establishing churches in Alexandria (*EH* 2:16). It is quite conceivable that, even if they had not traveled

---

3. Snape, "Peter and Paul," 130.
4. Snape, "Peter and Paul," 133.
5. Pearson, *Christians and Jews*, 207.
6. González, *A History*, 40.

together, their paths may have crossed as their missionary work overlapped in Alexandria.

The Acts of Peter offers significantly more detail of Peter's work in Rome, including the captivating *Quo Vadis* legend, than does the Acts of the Apostles.[7] Neither, however, offers verifiable details of his time spent or activities in Rome, or of his contributions to church establishment. There is some later anecdotal evidence, but no first-century document that tells us of Peter's work or his martyrdom in Rome.[8] As will be shown shortly, there may be a very logical historical reason why there are no extant records affirming Peter's role in the church in Rome. Regardless of the lack of verifiable evidence of his contributions to the emerging church in Rome, tradition and the writings of the early church fathers suggest that Peter was to some degree active in the church in Rome. Even if we accept Peter's active role in the church in Rome, we are left with the conundrum of how Peter's Jerusalem church theology interacted with (clashed with? contributed to?) the Hellenistic theology of Paul who, tradition holds, was also instrumental in the formation of the church in Rome. More to the point of our inquiry, how did Mark perceive the differences between the two theologies and how did that affect his Gospel?

Paul

If we are to consider Peter's influence on Mark's Gospel, we must also consider what influence Paul's ministry and theology had on the growing church in Rome. Paul's Hellenistic theology conflicted with that of the Jerusalem church, and both were met in Rome. The reality of Mark's world was that he would have been privy to the teachings, theology, and evangelical persuasions of both of these dominant church figures.

At the time Mark put together his Gospel, Paul's theology would have been neither codified, widely known, nor authoritative. Unfortunately, we have no idea how many of his letters have been lost, thus depriving us of a more in-depth understanding of his work and theology. Although there is some doubt as to how much time he spent in Rome, the Acts of the Apostles tells us that he had some involvement and influence on its growing Christian community. Acts ends with him leaving Caesarea under arrest and arriving in Rome around 62 CE to stand trial. Acts 28, however, portrays a man seemingly unrestricted and able to carry on his missionary work in Rome

---

7. *Domine quo vadis* ("Lord, where are you going?"), Peter asked of Jesus during the persecution. Jesus responded, "I am coming to Rome to be again crucified."

8. Snape, "Peter and Paul," 130.

for two more years. Sources generally agree with Eusebius (*EH* 2:25), that the martyrdom of Peter and Paul occurred in Rome during the Neronian persecution which could have been anytime between 65 to 69 CE. Once the rebellion in Judea started in 66 CE, it is likely that the fate of Peter and Paul, both from Judea and both teaching contrary to Rome's pagan tradition, was fatally sealed.

CHRISTIANITY IN ROME

What reasons could there have been for establishing a Christian church in Rome, the seat of power and authority of the empire, the center of pagan worship that was fundamental to Roman society? Looking back, it seems it would have been dangerous to establish a new relegion under the noses of the pagan imperial rulers, to whom loyalty to their imperial pagan gods was proof of loyalty to both empire and emperor. On the other hand, a church based in the imperial capital would assume an air of validity, power, influence, and authority.[9] Additionally, as the hub of the empire, Rome was vital to communication throughout that vast territory. As will be shown, a cascade of events placed the Hellenists in a most favorable position to strengthen their hold and influence on the church in Rome and eventually the entire Christian movement.

What little we know of Christianity in Rome in the first century comes to us more from informed conjecture than verifiable facts. Our best resources are smatterings of Christian and Roman records. Those records, especially the historical accounts written by Roman historians Suetonius and Tacitus, verify that there was an active Christian community in Rome. The Christian records from which we can gather some information about the formation and growing importance of the church in Rome include the Acts of the Apostles, Paul's Letter to the Romans, the Apocryphal Acts of Peter, and certain writings of the patristic church fathers written years later. Irenaeus, for example, tells us that "Peter and Paul were preaching at Rome, and laying the foundations of the Church" (*AH* 3.1.1).

Despite Irenaeus's and Eusebius's conclusions, the assumption that Peter and Paul were actively involved in founding the church in Rome is born more out of traditional suppositions than verifiable records. What traditional records we do have, written many years after the fact, shine only a dim light on the history of the church in Rome. This is understandable when we consider that those documents were not written to provide the chronological or factual accuracy of a historical record. Nonetheless, there

9. Bovon, "The Emergence," 25.

is evidence of a growing Christian church community intermingling itself among different social strata of the city's culture. In Romans 16:3–16 Paul commends several brothers and sisters to the church there, and throughout the Acts of Peter mention is made of Christian aristocrats and servants alike. This growing faction of Roman Christians would have been increasingly dominated by Gentiles with no attachment to either Judaism or the Jerusalem church, with little to no knowledge of Jewish religious traditions, and no ties of loyalty to Jerusalem.

There is little verifiable information regarding the journeys of the early Christians. With this in mind, we must again recognize how our schematic processing fills in gaps with facts not in evidence. While the Acts of the Apostles recognizes that journeys were made, it merely indicates journeys were made to already established Christian communities,[10] not who did the establishing or when they were established. Eusebius refers to considerable Jewish and Christian activities in Alexandria (*EH* 2:16–17), but neither Paul's letters nor the Acts of the Apostles details any Christian activity in that city with a large Jewish population and that rivaled Rome in importance. Actually, Rome itself fairs little better. While Rome was the seat of wealth and power within the empire, and a well-established church there would be advantageous for this new movement, we have no determinative evidence of the why, when, or by whom the church in Rome was first established.[11] Despite the scarcity of historical evidence of the founding and maintenance of the church in Rome, we may make some valid assumptions that collectively give us justifiable answers to certain pressing questions. As for "by whom?" and "when?," most likely it was founded by those Hellenistic Christians who fled Jerusalem after Stephen was martyred[12] (Acts 8:1), and obviously before 57 CE, the purported year Paul wrote his letter to the Roman church. Because the Romans incorporated much of the great Greek culture and religion into their own society, Hellenists, with their accrual of Greek language and culture, would have been well suited for assimilation into the city. Proselytes (non-Jews who converted to Judaism, many of whom continued their conversion to Christianity) probably fared well. As Gentiles they would have been better integrated into the city culture than Jews and, as non-Jews, may have escaped expulsion under Claudius's eviction order. As will be detailed shortly, in 49 CE Emperor Claudius expelled the Jews from Rome, thus casting a distrustful cloud over all things Jewish.

10. Bovon, "The Emergence," 24–25.

11. Eastman, "Jealousy," 40, fn 23.

12. Snape, "Christian Origins," 231, 243.

The resulting diminution of an active Jewish community in Rome marked an opening for the Hellenists to advance their control of the Roman church.

Roman records mention Christianity only incidentally to clarify some important Roman event or justify Rome's atrocious actions. For example, Suetonius tells us of Emperor Claudius's edict expelling all Jews from Rome in 49 CE, associating them with Christians: "Since the Jews constantly made disturbances at the instigation of Chrestus [Christ] he expelled them from Rome." [13] Acts 18:2 specifically mentions Claudius's order of expulsion as the reason for Priscilla and Aquila being in Corinth. Unfortunately, Suetonius does not give us the details of the disturbances he notes. We may deduce from Suetonius's statement that, at this point in history, the Christians were viewed as associated with the otherwise accepted Jews, perhaps as a Jewish sect. From that time forward, however, throughout the 50s, mistrust of Jews and—guilt by association—Christians grew in Rome.[14]

We can assume that Jews drifted back to Rome some years after Claudius's edict because in Romans 16:3 we find Prisca and Aquila back in Rome conducting a church. In the interim, however, given Roman resentment of Jews, Christian missionaries, especially Judaized Christians, would have been wise to be cautious in their work. We may surmise, however, that Hellenized Christians might have been better tolerated, especially if, like Paul, they were Roman citizens—which might explain why Paul had some liberty while awaiting his trial. With the Jews leaving Rome, it stands to reason that Hellenized Christians would gain further control of the Roman church. It would explain Luke's (Acts) rendering of a favorable reception for Paul by the believers on his arrival in Rome. It might also foretell the decline of the power and authority of the Jerusalem church and the ascendency of the Roman Church.

The fate of all Christians in Rome, however, took a brutal turn when a great fire engulfed Rome in 64 CE. Raging for several days it eventually burned ten of the city's fourteen districts.[15] Historical evidence points to Emperor Nero as the culprit arsonist but, through manipulation of his power, he escaped any involvement with the fire by placing blame on Christians.

---

13. Suetonius, *Lives*, 25. The Romans granted Jews considerable autonomy in Rome, even permitting them to govern their own section of the city (González, *A History*, 39). While they were exempt from persecution, expulsion, however, was an alternative.

14 The incident mentioned in Acts 16:19–24 is a good example of Roman attitudes toward the Jews. It occurs in Philippi, "a Roman colony," where Paul and Silas were seized by the mob and dragged before the magistrate. They were accused of "disturbing our city; they are Jews and are advocating customs that are not lawful for us as Romans to adopt or observe."

15. *Ann.* 15:40.

The best account we have of this disaster, Nero's duplicity, and subsequent consequences comes to us from Tacitus:

> But all human efforts, all the lavish gifts of the emperor, and the propitiations of the gods, did not banish the sinister belief that the conflagration was the result of an order. Consequently, to get rid of the report, Nero fastened the guilt and inflicted the most exquisite tortures on a class hated for their abominations, called Christians by the populace. Christus, from whom the name had its origin, suffered the extreme penalty during the reign of Tiberius at the hands of one of our procurators, Pontius Pilatus, and a most mischievous superstition, thus checked for the moment, again broke out not only in Judaea, the first source of the evil, but even in Rome, where all things hideous and shameful from every part of the world find their centre and become popular. Accordingly, an arrest was first made of all who pleaded guilty; then, upon their information, an immense multitude was convicted, not so much of the crime of firing the city, as of hatred against mankind. Mockery of every sort was added to their deaths. Covered with the skins of beasts, they were torn by dogs and perished, or were nailed to crosses, or were doomed to the flames and burnt, to serve as a nightly illumination, when daylight had expired (*Ann.* 15.44).

We can glean a lot information from Tacitus's account. First, unlike in 49 CE, Christians were now recognized as a distinct group (cult or sect) of worshippers, perhaps associated with Jews but, nonetheless, separate—and now a threat. Second, someone named Christus was the founding figure of this group in Judea, and he was known for being found guilty of a capital crime that led to his execution by order of Procurator Pontius Pilate. Third, indictment for arson was secondary to the primary indictment of "hatred of mankind." What did the Romans see that led them to believe that this was a faith hateful of mankind? Finally, many of the condemned Christians were victims of betrayal from within their own group.

As despicable and vicious as Nero's execution of Christians was, he was supported in his actions by none other than some Jews in Rome who colluded with the Roman authorities in betraying the Christians.[16] Tacitus's allusion to the offensive nature of Christians may have been prompted by Jewish propaganda. Reading multiple accounts of the events, attitudes, and actions of all the major players of that time period in Rome, it becomes obvious that a festering animosity and suspiciousness plagued

---

16. Snape, *"Christian Origins,"* 243.

their relationships. From the early Hellenist missionaries a community of Gentile Christians with minimal ties to or concern for Jewish orthodoxy would start to grow. The growing differences added to the emerging hostility between the two factions. Consider the following facts. Traditionally, the Romans made an exception for the Jews to remain culturally and religiously separate despite an imperial culture that demanded conformity. Starting in 49 CE, the activities of the Christians, whatever those activities might have been, suddenly upset the tolerant nature of that relationship. Although Claudius found Christian activities offensive, it was, by association, the Jews who became the target of his eviction order. Another wedge between the Jews and Christians was hammered home when Paul alienated the Jews in Rome (Acts 28:23–28). Politically, religiously, and culturally the Romans had good reason to suspect and dislike both Jews and Christians. The gods of Rome, including the emperor, were state gods. Loyalty to these gods was inherent in Roman culture; those not worshipping and sacrificing to those gods, for example, Jews and, increasingly, Christians, were risking divine retribution on the empire—and a fire that destroyed 90 percent of the city was direct evidence. Finally, in addition to the conflict between the Jews and Christians, there existed conflict within the Roman Christian church as well.

What knowledge we have of the early beginnings of the church in Rome is obfuscated by several factors, the fire and subsequent persecution in particular, but also, in no small measure, by distrust, duplicity, and discord within the Christian church itself.[17] Paul alludes to this conflict in Philippians 1:15, 17: "Some proclaim Christ from envy and rivalry, but others from goodwill . . . the others proclaim Christ out of selfish ambition not sincerely but intending to increase my suffering in my imprisonment." In 1 Clement, written around the turn of the first century CE, the author alludes to internal strife within the church that led to the deaths of Peter and Paul: "By reason of jealousy and envy the greatest and most righteous pillars of the Church were persecuted, and contended even unto death."[18] Not only did the Jews inform on the Christians but, according to Tacitus, the author of 1 Clement, and Paul, Christians were betraying one another. What would prompt them to do so? The answer to that question requires a deeper look into the conflict between the Judaizers and the Hellenists.

Soon after the crucifixion several traditions about Jesus arose as the believers tried to make sense of his life and, especially, his death. We do know that Christianity developed out of the fabric of orthodox Judaism.

17. Snape, "Peter and Paul," 129.
18. Clement, Letter.

It did not take long, however, before threads of Jesus movements began to unravel and pull in different directions. The term "Jesus movements" refers to any of several diverse groups that tried to claim interpretive and successor rights to the Jesus event. As in every case of cultural pluralism, divisions arose. Paul recognizes and addresses such divisions within the church in 1 Corinthians 11:18. The development of Christianity can only be hypothesized as we look back through the fog of history to find meaning in the nature of those complex divisions. Out of these disparate Jesus movements the two most prominent were the Judaizers of the Jerusalem church, and the Hellenistic Christ cult. The Judaizers acknowledged Jesus' messiahship, but within traditional Jewish orthodoxy, maintaining a strict adherence to the Mosaic law: "But some believers who belonged to the Pharisees stood up and said, 'It is necessary for them [Gentiles] to be circumcised and ordered to keep the law of Moses'" (Acts 15:5). The Hellenistic Christ cult held that Jesus brought freedom from the law, replacing it with the Holy Spirit: "But if you are led by the Spirit, you are not subject to the law" (Gal 5:18). While Jesus' messiahship was generally accepted[19] not all Jesus movements accepted his divinity.[20] The Hellenistic Christ cult embraced Jesus as both Messiah and as divine redeemer of humankind who not only died for our sins and was buried but was also raised from the dead—what has come to be the essential kerygma,[21] so essential that without it, according to Paul, "our proclamation . . . and your faith has been in vain" (1 Cor 15:14). The ensuing growth of the Christian communities was nourished by this kerygma.[22] It is difficult two thousand years removed to understand the intensity of the clash between the Jewish Jesus communities and the Hellenistic Christ cult. What we do need to understand is that the essence of modern Christianity grew out of that struggle.[23] Our present effort requires us to remain focused on how that struggle may have affected what Mark included and excluded in his narrative.

It would seem that the intra-church betrayals were fueled in part by the clash of primitive church ideologies. It is not unthinkable that the Hellenist bloc, which would have had more in common culturally with the Romans, and cautious to protect itself, would have felt little need to protect Jewish Christians. Additionally, the Jews were perturbed by both Christian factions

19. Kraus, "The Early Church," 259–60.

20. Mack, *A Myth,* 101

21 ". . . that Christ died for our sins in accordance with the scriptures, and that he was buried, and that he was raised on the third day in accordance with the scriptures" (1 Cor. 15:3–5).

22. England, "Tradition and Life," 81.

23. Kraus, "The Early Church," 252.

and would have found it advantageous to sell out either one or both groups to the Romans.[24] In the end the Jerusalem church was eliminated and, by default, the Hellenistic Christ cult assumed control. This may explain why there are no extant first-hand accounts and only unreliable secondary sources of Peter's role in the church of Rome. The Hellenists would be much less inclined to preserve the facts of the role played by the Jerusalem church in the beginnings of the church in Rome. There is one more extremely significant historical event that would add to this betrayal scenario—the first Roman-Jewish War that raged from 66 CE to 70 CE.

While neither the causes nor details of the first Jewish War, in and of themselves, are important to our Markan discourse at this time, the fact that it happened when it did and the end result significantly shape our understanding of Mark's world. In 66 CE the Romans felt compelled to militarily intervene to subdue certain serious insurrectionist activities in Judea and its environs. Emperor Nero chose Vespasian as commander of Roman forces. The war lasted four years, culminating with the siege and destruction of Jerusalem by Roman forces led by Vespasian's son Titus. This war came only two years after the fire in Rome, a fire Emperor Nero blamed on Christians who were thought to be associated with the Jews who were now in open rebellion against the empire. The war came during the Neronian persecutions of Christians and quite possibly exacerbated those persecutions. From a Roman perspective, what was to like about either of these religious cults? The Christians burned their city and the Jews were rebelling in Judea. The fire occurred in 64 CE, the Neronian persecutions started in 65, and the war in 66. If one lays those events one over another, it is easy to see the precarious position in which the church was placed. Considering that Jews in Judea were in open rebellion against the empire, the Jews in Rome would certainly want to distance themselves from any action that might be deemed anti-Roman—lending credence to the theory that the Jews betrayed the Christians. Furthermore, Hellenists would want to distance themselves from both Jews and Judaized Christians, giving validity to the premise that they willingly betrayed those associated with the Jerusalem church. That time period coincides with the accepted time span in which Peter and Paul were executed. There was sufficient animosity and treachery between all these factions to believe Peter and Paul were betrayed from within the church itself.[25]

How could any loyal Roman citizen distinguish between Jews in Rome, Jewish nationals in open rebellion, and Christians, a sect of Judaism

---

24. Acts 12:3 tells us that Herod (Agrippa) recognized that his execution of James "pleased the Jews," and he then felt emboldened to go after Peter. In other words, the Jews were not opposed to the elimination of these Christian leaders.

25. Snape, "Peter and Paul," 130; Cullmann, "Dissension Within," 90.

that worshipped as God a man who was executed for sedition in rebellious Judea? The Roman Empire was fighting an armed rebellion in the homeland of this alleged Jewish hero. Who could guarantee that rebellion would not be brought home to the capital city by those Jews or Christians loyal to these seditionist groups? (Consider America's actions against Japanese Americans after Pearl Harbor.) Neither the Empire nor its citizens would tolerate such a threat, far or near, to their country. All things Jewish and Christian were suspect among those hideous groups that found a home in Rome.

The war obliterated the Jewish nation. Its surviving citizens literally ran for their lives. Their culture was nearly erased. The destruction of the Temple, the symbol of a millennial-long connection to their God and their ancient religious past, would dramatically and forever change their religious practices And the same could be said for the Christian faith. With the destruction of Jerusalem came the destruction of the Jerusalem church and elimination of its authority. Its leaders were either dead or on the run. Christians, in general, were distrusted and ripe for betrayal. The physical destruction of the Temple had symbolic meaning as well, for it symbolized in dramatic fashion a severing with the old covenant as Paul had been preaching (see Heb 8:6) for years.[26] Judaism was the old covenant, and if the church in Rome, indeed, Christianity itself, was to survive, it would survive with a Pauline/Hellenist theology. The elimination of the Jerusalem church created a vacuum in leadership within the church at large. External threats and internal turmoil placed the Hellenist Roman church in position to fill that leadership vacuum. Paul was gone, but his theology was now unfettered from its Jerusalem church origins.

All members of the Roman church, from the leadership, to prominent Roman believers, to the lowliest slave, would have been affected by all of these events. And those events would profoundly influence Mark's narrative. Within the span of a few years Mark witnessed the death of Peter and Paul and the elimination of the Jerusalem church; losses so significant that Christianity's future was at risk. Being witness to all this loss, living on the edge of catastrophe and as a member of "a class hated for their abominations," Mark chose to create a narrative about the leader of this hated cult. Why?

---

26. Brandon, *The Trial of Jesus*, 63.

PART II

Literary Motifs and Martyrs

3

Gospel Origins

WHATEVER TRIUMPHS MARK WITNESSED in the growth and development of the early church the years from the mid-60s to the early 70s CE presented far more tragedies. Church leaders Peter and Paul executed; Jerusalem destroyed; the Jerusalem church and its de facto authority eliminated; Judea vanquished; the Temple, God's very house, razed; Rome and its gods triumphant over the Jewish nation and its God; the Roman Christian church threatened by internal strife and external scorn; and Christians and Jews alike living in fear of Roman retribution. Mark might have questioned whether or not the church in Rome, and Christianity itself, for that matter, had a future. Rather than yield to pessimism he, instead, responded by creating a document so unique and so sturdy as to serve as the corner stone for a religion destined to engulf the world. This chapter will examine the sources that were available to Mark upon which he could rationally build a meaningful narrative of Jesus. Those sources also reveal much about the nature of the primitive church. They include the oral and written traditions within the primitive church that preceded the Gospels, the elusive "Q" and other written documents, and Mark's audience, which served both as a source of information and a source of purpose. Before delving into all these sources, however, it is necessary to examine the priority of the Gospel according to Mark, that is, where it falls in the chronology of Gospel creation.

THE PRIORITY OF MARK

Mark's Gospel needs to be put into chronological perspective with regard to the other Gospels before proceeding on our exploration of his world. The similarities in the Gospels of Matthew, Mark, and Luke were noted many centuries ago. This led to the pursuit of a complex concern that came to be called the *Synoptic Problem*, essentially a formal way of asking: Why are these three Gospels, and just these three, for John's is markedly different, so much alike? This question leads to another: Where they are different, why are they different? The simple reasons for being alike is that either the Evangelists copied one another or they all copied a common source, or a combination of those two possibilities. Simply copying a common source would explain the similarities in their Gospels but not the differences. In the end, there is no simple solution to the Synoptic Problem.

Attempting to resolve the Synoptic Problem cannot be done without putting the Gospels into chronological order, which opens the centuries-long debate of proving the order of Gospel creation. That debate has sent Mark's Gospel on a roller coaster ride of priority acceptance in the Christian community. Initially, as the only narrative on the life of Jesus, it held unchallenged prominence in the primitive Christian church. That distinction was eventually challenged as the Gospels of Matthew and Luke became available.

Probably the earliest challenge to the priority of Mark came from Augustine of Hippo, who asserted that Mark copied Matthew in abbreviated form:

> Mark follows him [Matthew] closely, and looks like his attendant and epitomizer. For in his narrative he gives nothing in concert with John apart from the others: by himself separately, he has little to record; in conjunction with Luke, as distinguished from the rest, he has still less; but in concord with Matthew, he has a very large number of passages.[1]

Over the centuries the position of Mark in the chronology of Gospel creation has generated two major competing theories. The most widely held hypothesis, known as the *two-source theory*, holds that Mark and the elusive Q source (discussed below) were the models for Matthew and Luke.[2] The most prominent argument against the priority of Mark, however, one that still maintains limited scholarly traction, was launched in 1776 by J.J. Griesbach who held that Matthew wrote first, Luke copied Matthew, and Mark

---

1 Augustine, "De consensus evangelistrarum," 1.2.4.

2. Osborne, *The Hermeneutical Spiral*, 201; Dibelius, *From Tradition*, 233. Lührmann, "The Gospel of Mark," 51–52.

copied them both.[3] Acceptance of the *Griesbach hypothesis* has waxed and waned over the centuries but in the end the priority of Mark is now the most widely-accepted theory.[4] Although it is now commonly accepted that Mark was the first Gospel written, the reason it was written at that time and in that form still eludes us.

Establishing the priority of any of the gospels is not simply an academic exercise, a scholarly prize without wider consequences. Each gospel, regardless of its similarities, delivers a different message, offers different theological insights, and projects a glimpse into the spiritual purpose, hopes, and aspirations of its particular writer. Once we accept the priority of Mark we can see deeper into his world and, consequently, the world of the early Christian church. We can begin to see what he saw as the needs of his church, a church beset by social, religious, and political forces and in need of validation of its faith in this Galilean who was ignominiously executed for sedition and who definitely did not fit their long embedded schema of a Messiah. Mark had his work cut out!

PRE-MARKAN TRADITIONS

We noted previously that in addition to the study of the situation, the *Sitz im Leben*, of the writers of the four Gospels (redaction criticism), New Testament scholars also engage in the study of another type of situation, that of the traditional methods, oral and written, used to pass on the story of Jesus during the period from the resurrection up to the first written Gospel. This is known as *form criticism*. By identifying certain patterns in the history of the tradition, form criticism seeks to identify patterns of use as a way to understand how the traditional material functioned within the life of the community.[5] Not only do we need to learn how the traditional material affected the lives of its audience but also how the audience affected the content and the methods used to pass on that content. Mark made use of the existing sources (besides Peter's sermons), scattered and unconnected as they may have been, that informed the primitive church community of the life and work of Jesus. So what was available to him? That question leads to an array of hypotheses—some more persuasive than others. There was not a single encapsulated pre-Markan tradition from which Mark could gain guidance and scholars still dispute what exactly preceded the first Gospel.

---

3. Stein, *Studying*, 50, 125.

4. Osborne, *The Hermeneutical Spiral*, 201; Dawsey, *Peter's Last Sermon*, 15

5. Koester, "One Jesus," 204.

Once we accept the priority of Mark it becomes obvious that he had neither the Gospel of Matthew nor Luke available to him as a source model. It is likely that Luke's recognition at the beginning of his Gospel that others "have undertaken to set down an orderly account of the events that have been fulfilled" (1:1), is a reference to Mark's Gospel. If Mark had no organized written account of Jesus' life on which to base his work, then what was available to him to create a narrative about Jesus that would be so formidable as to achieve the status of *Gospel* and so enduring that it would arguably become the most researched book in the New Testament?

As late as the 60s CE there was no organized narrative of the earthly ministry of Jesus; there only existed independent stories lacking chronological connectedness.[6] The only story that was commonly shared that contained consistent chronological features was the Passion Narrative, which will be discussed in detail in chapter 8.[7] The absence of an organized narrative of Jesus' life was one thing; it was quite another that not even the idea of creating such a narrative could or should be attempted. There was neither precedent nor model for creating such a narrative and, absent the Jerusalem church, no authority for creating one. Undeterred, Mark would give the Christian community an account of the life, actions, miraculous deeds, prayers, teachings, sayings, and warnings in order to validate Jesus as the Christ. What a task! Pretend, for a moment, that you are Mark. Where do you start? What is "out there" that you can use as a resource? How do you write a message of belief in a world where that belief is generally ridiculed and despised? Who is the audience for whom you write? What is the story you want to tell? Mark/you would have to consider all those questions before beginning.

Oral Tradition

The oral tradition refers to that period of time when information was almost exclusively transmitted by word of mouth rather than written down. It is ironic that the only path open for us to explore the oral tradition is through the written records that have survived the ages. In the first century those who were literate[8] could be divided into two groups: those who were only functionally literate; that is, they could read and write enough to sustain

6. Dibelius, *From Tradition*, 178; Stein, "The Proper Method," 195.

7. Many scholars contend that the gospels themselves are simply long introductions to the Passion Narrative, (Wallis, "Why Mark Wrote," 47).

8. About 2 to 5 percent, mostly among men and the elite class, (Dewey, "The Gospel of Mark," 7).

their work; and those whose literacy afforded them perceptive engagement with a wide array of written material.[9] Today the terms "literacy" and "illiteracy" carry judgmental overtones: literacy is good, illiteracy, while not bad, is not as good. We should be careful not to allow our modern definition of literacy influence our perception of Mark's first-century audience. After all, Acts 4:13 tells us that Peter and John were "uneducated ordinary men." This could mean that they were ordinary men who happened to be uneducated, or that the common ordinary man at that time was uneducated. Most likely it was the latter. Regardless, both were quite successful in spreading the Word. Given that the oral tradition preceded the written tradition, it seems logical that stories of Jesus within the primitive church were passed on both orally and in writing. The driving force behind the continuing transmission of the Jesus stories was to promote a singular confession of faith, a kerygma, that Jesus was the Messiah, the "good news" sent by God the Father.[10]

The oral transmission of information was preferred during the first and early second centuries CE. Eusebius wrote of Papias' claim that whenever he met

> . . . a follower of the elders anywhere, I made it a point to inquire over the declarations of the elders. What was said by Andrew, Peter or Philip. By Thomas, James, John, Matthew, or any other of the disciples of our Lord . . . for I do not think that I derive so much benefit from books as from the living voice of those that are still surviving (E H 3:39).

Papias' attitude reflects a general first-century cultural mistrust of the written word.[11]

What at first in Mark appears to be poor writing style and grammar may be the result of someone trying to copy verbatim what is heard in a sermon or storytelling, that is, it reflects the common way we speak rather than the way we would write.[12] The compiler would have collected the verbatim copies and the editor, unlike editors today, would then publish them without correction. Or a single author would have collected them and arranged them to meet his purpose, again without contextualizing them into a consistently articulate narrative. The Gospels have been grammatically updated so often to the prevailing standards of the times that we now see few of the syntactical defects of the original narratives.

9. Dixon, "Descending Spirits," 765, fn 28.
10. Piper, "The Origin," 121–22; Reedy, "About the Kerygma," 353.
11. Dawsey, Peter's Last Sermon, 9, 11.
12. Guy, The Origin, 74; Bilezikian The Liberated Gospel, 115.

A strong oral tradition was common in the Hellenic culture, with its long tradition of memorization and oral transmission of great works such as those of Homer.[13] This preference for the oral over the written word can be traced back to Socrates: "Then anyone who leaves behind him a written manual, and likewise anyone who takes it over from him, on the supposition that such writing will provide something reliable and permanent, must be exceedingly simple-minded."[14] It is likely that the Jewish culture's preference for the spoken over the written word was strongly influenced by its Hellenistic roots.

The oral tradition in the Hellenist period dates from ca. 330 to 30 BCE, and the Roman period from ca. 30 BCE. to 476 CE.[15] Not only was Mark a product of a culture steeped in nearly 400 years of a strong oral tradition before he wrote his Gospel, but he was also the recipient of stories told and re-told over and over for nearly forty years, first in Aramaic, then in Greek, and perhaps some in Latin. Cultural studies have proven that no story can sustain accuracy when exposed to even a few such influential factors. Oral transmission of stories leans more toward being emotionally persuasive rather than factual.[16] Aristotle, perhaps, recognized this when he wrote: "The orator persuades by means of his hearers, when they are roused to emotion by his speech."[17] Stories are told for a purpose, and, as the purpose changes from teller to teller, so, too, does the story. The discrepancies among the four Gospels regarding the same event or pericope suggests that each Evangelist "heard" different versions of that story or slanted the story to stress his own theological perspective. Mark had to sort through various versions to come up with a final written narrative that not only fit his purpose but would also convince an audience that placed more faith in a story told than in a story read. This was another hurdle for Mark to clear.

Written Tradition

There is no doubt that a strong oral tradition existed in the primitive church and initially played a major role in the transmission of the Jesus stories. There are, however, obvious inherent problems with oral transmission, not the least of which are lack of consistency and accuracy. Additionally, there is, like gossip, no fixed source; therefore no one accountable to validate the

13. Aune, "Prolegomena," 66–68.

14. Plato, "Phaedrus," (275 c), 249.

15. Aune, "Prolegomena," 60.

16. Dewey, "The Gospel of Mark," 8.

17. Aristotle, *Rhetoric*, 1.2.4.

truth of the story. In the earliest years of the Christian church, such referral duties fell to the surviving apostles and the Jerusalem church, but by 70 CE those apostolic leaders and the Jerusalem church were gone. The written record, despite Socrates' objections, has obvious advantages over the oral narrative. It is a consistent account of what happened, thus making one un-changed story available to a widespread audience. And it can be attributed to a particular source to corroborate or disprove accuracy. It was inevitable, then, that the sayings, miracle anecdotes, and pericopes of the Jesus event would be, had to be, written down. Today Christians rely on the massed col-lection of written works (for example, the Canonical texts) to anchor their profession of faith, but in the first century those written works were few in number, scattered, unconnected, and considered suspect.

WRITTEN SOURCES

The Q Source

Perhaps the earliest written text of significance is what has come to be known as "the Q document." By the mid-eighteenth century it was recog-nized that some common source existed in the early church community long before the gospels. It was initially called *Logia*,[18] but has since become known as the Q document, Q being short for *Quelle*, German for *source*. As the source gained attention it gained other designations as well, such as the Source Q,[19] or Synoptic Sayings Source "Q."[20] To complicate matters further, it is speculated that there were two nearly, but not entirely, identical Q docu-ments. One, designated simply as Q, was used by the Eastern churches, and the other, designated Q^R, was used by the Roman church.[21]

Leading Christian scholars and theologians have come to accept the existence of Q, but no one knows if this source was a page, a loose collection of pages, or a scroll. For the most part, the Q document consists of the say-ings of Jesus,[22] giving rise to the "Sayings Source" description. There is no Passion Narrative nor any reflection upon Jesus' death in Q,[23] nor is there any mention of Jesus as Messiah.[24] The fact that Q lacks any kerygmatic

18. Kloppenborg and Vaage, "Early Christianity," 2.

19. Castor, "The Relation of Mark," 82.

20. Koester, "One Jesus," 208.

21. Honey, "Did Mark use Q?" 319, 329.

22. Head and Williams, "Q Review," 120.

23. Kloppenborg, "The Sayings Gospel Q," 331; Mack, "Q and the Gospel," 19.

24. Mack, "Q and the Gospel," 19.

theme strongly suggests that theologically the Christian faith started down a distinctly different path from its traditional Pauline Hellenistic Christ cult existence.[25] As a "Sayings Source," Q is much like the Gospel of Thomas that we will review shortly.

Although neither fragments of the Q source exist nor was such a source referred to by the early church fathers,[26] that such a source did exist has been determined by the recognition of numerous sections in the Gospels of Matthew and Luke—but not Mark—that are strikingly similar in wording and phrasing.[27] Many years of research led to a delineation of several of these instances which have been codified into the Q Source. One such example is the Beelzebub story in Matthew 12:22–32 and Luke 11:14–23 compared to Mark 3:22–30.[28] Beginning with Schleiermacher in 1832 and through Bultmann in the early twentieth century, so many scholars have demonstrated the existence of Q that there is no need to review those findings here.[29] Our understanding of the Q Source and its possible influence on Mark is essential. For one thing, if the Q Source existed, then the priority of Mark is validated.[30] Moreover, the Q document is crucial to understanding Christian origins.[31] Lastly, Mark's audience would have been exposed to this source for years before he wrote his Gospel and, thus, would have judged Mark accordingly. For now we need to focus on whether or not Mark would have had this document available to him and whether or not he used it.

Mark and Q

The Q document theory is fascinating and opens up a challengingly new perspective on the primitive church, the Gospels, and Christian theology. To go into detail here would be needlessly daunting and lead us astray from answering: Did Mark know of and use the Q document? If Q existed, no matter in what form, it would have been available for Mark as a source. As for the second part (Did Mark use the Q document?) the answer is complex

25. Vassaliadis, "Beyond Theologia Crucis," 140.

26 Although something in Papias's testimony triggered the earliest mid-eighteenth century investigations that eventually led to the Q source hypothesis, (Kloppenborg and Vaage, "Early Christianity," 2).

27. Head and Williams, "Q Review," 120.

28. Castor, "The Relation of Mark," 83; Honey, "Did Mark use Q?" 321–322.

29 Additional information on the Q document may be found online at the International Q Project: https://biblicalstudiesonline.wordpress.com/tag/international-q-project/.

30. Head and Williams, "Q Review," 120.

31. Mack, "Q and the Gospel," 15; Kloppenborg and Vaage, "Early Christianity," 1, 4.

and, like so many of these issues, impossible to prove. Although there seems to be no convincing consensus among scholars, it seems more than likely that if Q existed, a prominent leader in the church, such as Mark, would have been well aware of its contents.

While insights into Mark's world and the dynamics of the primitive Christian community are not dependent on validation of the existence of Q, its contents, or Mark's use of it, such validation would significantly contribute to our understanding of that world. Having access to Q would have given Mark another important perspective on the tradition of his church community and would have directly influenced his Gospel.[32] If, like many scholars, we accept that Mark did use Q or a variant thereof, then his Gospel gives us a glimpse back to Jesus as the earliest Christian community perceived him. Mark plus Q give us a deeper insight into the Christological *Sitz im Leben* of the primitive church.[33]

The Gospel of Thomas

Like Q, Thomas is a pre-Markan sayings source containing sayings of Jesus that are quite similar to those found in the Synoptic Gospels.[34] Factually, we know Thomas and Q predated Mark and were available to him as sources. How much Mark was influenced by either of these sources remains an open question.

The Didache

The Didache, also known as "The Teaching of the Twelve Apostles," is included in the short list of recognized apostolic writings outside the New Testament.[35] Considered the very first catechism of the church, its purpose, besides offering some ethical teaching, was to establish written instructions on such ritualistic procedures as baptism, fasting, and the Eucharist. Scholarship places its origin in the late first to early second century CE. The Didache is of utmost value in revealing the developing nature of rituals and law within the early church and where we first see a movement away from

32. Even if Mark rejected Q, such rejection would have influenced what he put in and left out of his Gospel.

33. Lührmann, "The Gospel of Mark," 53.

34. Koester, "One Jesus," 213.

35. Others include *Clement of Rome, Ignatius of Antioch, Polycarp of Smyrna, Papias of Hierapolis,* the *Epistle of Barnabas,* the *Sheppard of Hermas,* and the *Epistle to Diognetus,* (Gonzàlez, *A History,* 67).

apostolic church leadership to that of bishops and deacons.[36] Due to the uncertainty of a date of origin it is impossible to know whether or not Mark would have known of or had access to the Didache. While it is possible that he never saw anything in an organized written fashion it is conceivable that he was familiar with its individual contents before they were codified. It remains another open question on whether or not Mark was influenced by this document.

CHURCH LEADERS

If we accept the traditional conclusion that Mark was Peter's interpreter, then we must recognize that Mark had the advantage of hearing from one of the original apostles, one who was perhaps Jesus' closest confidant. Referring back to Eusebius's contention that Mark was Peter's interpreter, it follows that the first Christians believed that Mark was more or less repeating sermons from Peter himself. Additionally, Mark would have been privy to the teachings of James and Paul. Although Paul's letters were not yet codified in any semblance of organization as we know them today, if Mark traveled with Paul on those missionary journeys he would have been well acquainted with Paul's theological perspective. In short, he could have obtained the gist of his information on Jesus' earthly ministry from Peter, and other central church leaders such as Paul, James, and the other apostles. That group itself would have been a fount of information, and over the decades from that fount would have flowed a torrent of sermons, messages, and stories, mostly spoken but also some written, about the historical Jesus. Mark's task, then, was to gather as many of those scattered and unrelated resources as possible in an effort to create a written narrative of Jesus that would serve as a source for his church. If Mark was not secretary to Peter or knew any of the apostles, then he was tasked with gathering a wide array of material from numerous and diverse sources going back nearly forty years.

MARK'S AUDIENCE

Mark's audience served not only as the target of purpose but also as an important source of information. And just who was Mark's audience? This question will be examined in more detail in the next chapter. Generally, his initial audience included a broad spectrum of Jews and Gentiles, some hearing the narrative for the first time; others, the converted believers, would

36. Jerome, *The New Jerome Biblical Commentary*, 1348, 8:42.

have been familiar with some of the events about which Mark wrote. We should, then, be able to confidently say that these believers shared a common belief, but such is not the case. It is wrong to think that the primitive church was singular, static, fixed, consistent, or coherent in its faith and practice. That there was a plurality of early Christian groups with diverse beliefs is attested to by the variety of Christian documents within the New Testament.[37]

To understand Mark's Gospel one must recognize the great diversity, in some instances a diversity with opposing views, that existed in Mark's Christian world. We have already shown that there was a group descended from the Jerusalem church which was in conflict with the Hellenistic Christ cult. Thrown into the mix were the Gnostics, Docetists, Ebionites, and Nazareans.[38] Although obscure to us today, these groups were prominent and influential in the early days of the Christian movement. Additionally, the Judaizers in Rome likely practiced differently than the Judaizers in Alexandria, and both of those differently from those in Palestine. All of these believers responded to the historic Jesus differently in belief, faith, and ritual. There was not yet a "church" with formal unifying creeds or orthodoxy. Mark's challenge was to draw from that diversity of beliefs a unifying story that would convince the believers that Jesus was the Messiah.

Each Gospel reflects the era of its writing, and the era of its writing would influence what is written. Mark would have had to contend with the fact that the *Sitz im Leben* of the early church was diverse. In his search for what information was factual and what was made up, or at least embellished, he was faced with the fact that world events shaped certain memories of Jesus. As Mark surveyed this diverse collection within the primitive church he would have found conflicting beliefs and theologies serving as a wellspring of information. How does one write a Gospel for such a pluralistic group?

Considering all the pre-existing tradition sources it seems likely that Mark collected both oral and written tradition material. Such material included oral sermons delivered by preachers, which were recalled either from memory or from notes taken; it would include the sayings sources; and it would include whatever written information—sermons, sayings, anecdotes—was available. At some point he proceeded to compile all this information, perhaps with the intention of producing a coherent whole narrative that put Jesus' life in perspective or perhaps handing it off to someone else to complete that task. Despite the existing diversity of information, the

---

37. Bovon, *The Emergence*, 17.

38 At his hearing before Ananias, Paul was accused of being a "ringleader of a sect of the Nazarenes" (Acts 24:5); this term is not well defined.

kerygma was gaining strength as the unifying factor, especially within the Christ cult of the Hellenized church. Coming to grips with just who Jesus was, what he taught, his relationship to the religious beliefs and aspirations of a conquered Jewish nation would be difficult. When we ask, Why did Mark write this Gospel when he did?, we can add to the list of theories that perhaps he saw the believers struggling to make sense of Jesus as the Christ and decided that it was time to deliver the good news.

4

Mark's Gospel As Literature

UP TO THIS POINT we have examined those social, political, and religious events of the first century that would have most influenced Mark's story of Jesus. Mark wrote in the first century according to first-century literary motifs. It is important to know what role written literature played in the culture, beliefs, and attitudes of that era. This chapter will examine Mark's Gospel as a work of literature; its genre and how it fit into the literature of the first century, the characteristics and literary customs of his audience, and the dominating Greek literary influence on both Roman and Jewish literature. Here it is important to separate the written literary story being told from its kerygmatic theological message, which will be discussed in a later chapter.

FIRST-CENTURY READING AND WRITING

Essential to a comprehensive understanding of Mark we must understand its status as literature. To do so we must first examine that most fundamental aspect of literacy—*reading*. Reading, as we understand the term today, would have been rather bizarre to even a well-educated citizen in the first century. Their schema of interaction with written texts was wholly different from that of modern day readers. Not only was the written word generally suspect, but it was also interacted with differently. Written texts were read out loud even if the reader was alone.[1] The practice of reading a written work silently, as we nearly always do today, did not become a norm until near the end of the Middle Ages.[2] In biblical times it was expected that written texts would be read aloud; therefore, in preparing his written narrative, it would have been beyond Mark's comprehension to think individuals, whether in a group or in private, would read silently.[3] Indeed, Mark knew his audience as *hearers* not *readers*, a fact that influenced what he wrote and the syntax of his writing.[4]

Unlike the mass-produced bound scriptural texts we have today, first-century texts would have been individual handwritten scrolls limited in availability, difficult to mass produce, and too expensive for the common population. Mark wrote his Gospel with the understanding that it would be read aloud by one person in a gathered group. Reading selected passages would have been tedious, if not impossible. The normal practice would have been for a *Methurgeman*, an interpreter for an important rabbi in the Jewish synagogue who passed on his master's message,[5] what today we would call a lector, to give an oral interpretation of the entire Gospel from beginning to end at one sitting.[6] (Imagine how that would go over with your Sunday worship service today).

Mark wrote his Gospel in all capital letters with no breaks between words and with no punctuation.[7] So the entire Gospel manuscript would have looked something like this:

WHENHERETURNEDTOCAPERNUMAFTERSOMEDAYSIT-
WASREPORTEDTHATHEWASATHOMESOMANYGATHERE-
DAROUNDTHATTHEREWASNOLONGERROOMFORTHEM-
NOTEVENINFRONTOFTHEDOORANDPEOPLECAME-
BRINGINGTOHIMAPARALYZEDMANCARREDBYFOUROFT-
HEM (Mark 2:1–3).[8]

---

1. Stein, "Is Our Reading," 68. An example can be found in Acts 8:30 where Philip *heard* the eunuch reading from Isaiah.

2. Dawsey, *Peter's Last Sermon*, 9; Dewey, *The Gospel of Mark*, 7.

3. Stein, "Is Our Reading," 68.

4. Stein, "Is Our Reading," 68; Dawsey *Peter's Last Sermon*, 9

5. Guy, *The Origin*, 80, 144.

6. Dawsey, *Peter's Last Sermon*, 14.

7. Dawsey, *Peter's Last Sermon*, 13; Stein, "Is Our Reading," 71; Dewey, "The Gospel of Mark," 7.

8 The modern standard division of chapters was not added until the 1400s. Verse designation was not added until the late 1500s, not for theological reasons but to standardize the printing process (Dawsey, *Peter's Last Sermon*, 13, fn 19).

Without punctuation, those listening to someone reading the Gospel had no idea what the author wanted to emphasize or subordinate, no way to know where a thought began or ended, or how he wanted a particular word or phrase inflected. With no punctuation, the listening audience was at the mercy of the reader; thus, whatever Mark meant to convey in his Gospel was subject to the reader's interpretation.

Hearing the Gospel in its entirety made it difficult to focus on a specific passage, and it discouraged examination and discussion of parables, pericopes, or specific teachings within the Gospel narrative. Trying to comprehend the message from an entire Gospel at once rather than from its individual parts seems strange to us today, which is one of the factors that differentiates what we hear (comprehend) in Mark's Gospel from what his first-century audience heard. Our modern schematic paradigm of scriptural connotation impedes our hearing Mark as his original audience heard him. A further impediment to our understanding of Mark is the fact that we are recipients of the numerous differing translations of Mark's Greek into the Latin of the Vulgate and other ancient Bible texts to modern NIV, NRSV, KJV, etc, to different Catholic and Protestant Canonical texts and denominational theologies that influence what we "think" Mark wrote from what he actually wrote. This leads to a rigidity of schematic conviction resulting in the unsupported conclusion: "This is what Mark meant!" Such a conviction provides exegetical comfort, a means to justify our personal schema of what the Scripture *should* say. Unfortunately, the evidence used to endorse such a conviction is seldom verifiable.

Mark's Audience as Receivers

The last chapter ended with a look at how Mark's audience served as a source, a repository, of traditional material for his Gospel. Now we must consider the other side of the proverbial coin by looking at Mark's audience as the intended receiver. Mark had to take into account the cultural, linguistic, and historical characteristics of this first-century audience if he wanted his story to be understood. Much may be ascertained about his intended audience by using his Gospel as evidence of certain facts.

Mark, a Jew, wrote in Koine Greek about a Jewish miracle worker who he thought to be the long awaited Messiah. Those facts permit us to assume that his intended audience included Orthodox Jews, Hellenistic Jews, and Gentiles. Mark wrote simply and directly in order to fit the comprehension level of his *listening* audience. He wrote with an economy of style and language that allowed both literate and illiterate alike to gain an understanding of the Jesus event.[9]

Mark's Jewish audience would certainly have had knowledge of the Old Testament. They did not need explanations of who the Pharisees and scribes were, or what the Sanhedrin was, or what daily life under Roman rule was like. They knew the religious and historical significance of Moses and Elijah, and the sacredness of the Sabbath and the Temple. The Jewish audience would be familiar with such Old Testament expressions as "Son of Man," "Son of David," and other OT references. The fact that Mark wrote in Koine Greek indicates he had a wider audience in mind. While he uses many Aramaic expressions, he shows consideration for his non-Aramaic audience by translating certain Aramaic expressions, such as, "'*Talitha cum!*' which means, 'Little girl, get up.'" (5:41); "'*Eloi, Eloi, lama sabachthani?*' which means, 'My God, my God, why have you forsaken me?'" (15:34); and "'*Ephphatha,*' that is, 'Be opened.'" (7:34).[10] Another example is: "*Corban,* that is, an offering to God" (7:11); and "*Bonerges,* that is Sons of Thunder" (3:17). At 7:3–4 Mark digresses to explain the requirement according to the Law to wash hands, food, and cooking utensils before eating—a point all Jews would have known well. Mark's Greek-reading audience understood the cultural nuances and symbols of that language that added a depth to his narrative that is beyond modern comprehension. Jews and Gentiles alike were well versed in the myths and legends that were ubiquitous in their respective cultures and that Mark often used as background to some of his narrative's episodes.

Mark literally introduced the Jesus Christ we know (or think we know) to the primitive church (and subsequently to the world). From the second century on, Christians have been exposed to four Gospels and numerous teachings about Jesus. To Mark's first audience, however, his narrative was unique; there was nothing with which to compare it, and therefore nothing to influence its thinking. Those in the Jewish communities and the Hellenist bloc knew the long-existing, albeit diverse, oral and written tradition stories about Jesus; some quite possibly heard it from those with first-hand knowledge of Jesus himself. Mark must have known that any significant deviation from those traditional stories, especially the Passion Narrative, would have made the audience suspicious of his Gospel as a whole.

Mark and his audience shared a historic moment in time. Along with the pre-existing tradition stories came a worldview, a collective unconscious

9. Reminiscent of how Shakespeare could construct a narrative to be understood by both his Anglo-Saxon and Anglo-Norman audiences (McCrum R., et al., *The Story of English*, 84).

10. Beattie and Davies, "What does Hebrew Mean?," 72.

schema, of their God's (or gods') historic role, relationship, and interaction with humanity as instilled by either their Jewish or pagan culture. Mark had to align his worldview of Jesus with the worldview of his audience and resolve any discrepancies. That first-century worldview is as alien to us today as is Koine Greek. What we do not know of that time, what we cannot prove with facts, we all too often fabricate to fill the gaps with our twenty-first century schemas. For first-century Christians, the ones for whom Mark wrote, the gospel experience, the sum total of intellectual, spiritual, theological, and philosophical meaning, was substantially different from what it is for a twenty-first century audience.

Mark had to write within the historic context of his time, and the most significant event of that time was the Judean revolt against the Roman Empire. Those calling themselves Christians were especially suspect because their presumed founder had been executed for sedition against the empire. A similar fate had just recently been meted out to a few of their acknowledged leaders. As a matter of survival this audience, suspect in the eyes of the surrounding Jewish and Roman community, needed to exist on the fringes of society. Mark had to write so as to maintain their faith without further agitating or fueling the suspicions of the wider community—especially the Romans.

Gospel as Genre

The term *literary genre* (or literary form) refers to the category, based on form and style, by which a written work may be classified. *Moby Dick* would fall into the general genre of fiction. Within the fiction genre, it is also a *novel*. Moreover, because of its endurance over time as a superbly written piece of fiction, it has attained the additional quality of *classical* literature. Further, because of its excellent and exciting storyline and characterizations, it has achieved *epic* status, and, in numerous ways, it is a *tragedy*. Shakespeare's *Romeo and Juliet,* would share such literary characteristics as fiction, classical, and tragedy, but as a play, not a novel. *Savage Beauty: The Life of Edna St. Vincent Millay* would be classified as non-fiction and a biography. So a written piece of work can be classified and sub-classified depending on many factors. Although Melville is recognized for his novels and Shakespeare for his plays, both of them had hundreds of written works created over the previous centuries serving as examples for their writing. Mark did not have that advantage. Where Matthew, Luke, and John followed Mark's pattern, Mark created from scratch. While the term *euaggelion = the good news = gospel* was not unusual in the first century, it did not exist as a literary genre until Mark created his narrative.[11] The corpus of the gospel genre is quite small and difficult to define. Considering only the four gospels in the New Testament, we would like to think they are purely non-fiction but that is not entirely true. But then, neither are they fiction. They are not history in that they do not follow a systematic chronology complete with verifiable factual details. Nor are they biographies—to say otherwise would be stretching the meaning of biography, at least as we have come to understand that term, because they contain so very little detail about the life of Jesus. The Gospels are a genre unique unto themselves.[12]

GREEK LITERARY INFLUENCE

Historically, two stories have dominated the world of literature—that of Ulysses's protracted death-defying seafaring journey home, and that of a crucified god.[13] This is certainly true in Mark's case. Although Mark's Gospel would be a new form of literature, he was not totally deprived of literary examples, for his world offered a historically magnificent line of Greek literature from which to choose. The quintessence of literary work in Mark's world was to be found in Greek literature, not in Jewish texts. Our understanding of Mark's world and his Gospel will be enhanced by recognizing the dominance of the Greek literary tradition of that era.

Looking back over the expanse of the literary cosmos, the number of written works seems as countless as the stars in the night sky. For Mark, however, that number would not have been quite so dazzling. Although the number of written works available to even a very literate first-century inhabitant of the Roman empire was relatively small, that limitation made what was available profoundly influential—and nearly all those important works were Greek or based on historic Greek works. They included first and foremost Homer's great epics the *Odyssey* and the *Iliad*. The *Odyssey*, the most imitated book of the ancient world,[14] and other Homeric works were fundamental to education.[15] There were also the works of renowned philosophers such as Heraclitus, Xenophon, Pythagoras, Plato, and, especially, Aristotle's classic treatise *Poetics* ("On the Art of Poetry"). And before there

11. Dawsey, *Peter's Last Sermon*, 41; Bultmann, *History*, 348.

12. If anything, the Gospels are most similar to *Aretalogies*, that is, stories of divine men, that were common in the first century (Liefeld, "The Hellenistic 'Divine Man,'" 202). This will be discussed in Chapter 9.

13. Borges, "The Gospel According to Mark," 9.

14. MacDonald, *The Homeric Epics*, 5.

15. Dixon, "Descending Spirits," 765, fn 28.

was a Rome, there was the Greek stage. The plays with which even ordinary citizens, literate or not, may have been familiar would have been those of the three major Greek tragic dramatists: Aeschylus, Euripides, and Sophocles. One did not have to know how to read to understand the drama, most often tragic, being performed on stage. What the individual owed to the divine power(s), to his nation, his moral duty, his place and purpose in the cosmos all were strongly influenced by the Greek worldview—a worldview that permeated the fabric of Jewish thought and society. If we are to understand Mark's world and his gospel as it relates to that world we have to recognize the influence of the Greek literary style.

Upon conquering what remained of the great Alexandrian empire (ca. 168 BCE), Rome assimilated much of Greek culture into its own, not only its art and religion but also its literary style and accomplishments. Greek literature was the foundation of Hellenist and, consequently, Roman, Jewish, and Christian literature.[16] The great Roman poet Virgil (70 BCE to 19 BCE) produced a poetic makeover of the *Odyssey* and *Iliad* by combining the two stories into the *Aenead*. Rome was saturated with Greek works, especially the Homeric epics, the *Odyssey* and *Iliad*, as well as the works of the great Greek tragedians. In order to introduce Roman students to Greek history and culture, Livius Andronicus (284 BCE. to 204 BCE), a freed Greek slave turned influential Roman educator, translated Homer's *Odyssey* from the original Greek into the Latin *Odusia* and also translated the plays of Aeschylus, Euripides, and Sophocles, all best known for their great tragic dramas.[17] The Greek literary influence followed the spread of the Roman Empire and Hellenic culture. An archeological discovery at Miletus, a city in Asia Minor, revealed that first-century Jews also availed themselves of the theater. A row of seats discovered in an unearthed amphitheater there bears the inscription: "Place of the Jews, who are also called God-fearing."[18] If Jewish theater-going was so regular as to have earned them a row of reserved seats in the amphitheater in Miletus, we may safely conclude that the litany of Greek dramas was familiar to them.

The number of theaters or extent of theater-going in first-century Palestine, Galilee, or Syria is not the point. What is important is the fact that the Greek dramatic motif, especially the ideal of the martyr suffering, enduring, succumbing to, and finally triumphant over tragedy was inculcated into the worldview of first-century Jews, Hellenized or not. Such a worldview would

---

16. Bilezikian, *The Liberated Gospel,* 17.

17. Ricoeur (Symbolism of Evil, 212), notes that "the Greek example, in showing us the tragic itself, has the advantage of revealing to us . . . its connection with theology."

18. Deissmann, *Light,* 446 in Williams, *Jesus' Death,* 193.

have been shared by Mark and his audience. That worldview would be assimilated into their literature, politics, religion, and culture. One of the finest eras of Roman literary output started during Tiberius's reign (ca. 14 CE) and continued through the first century, a time that included the writing of the books of the New Testament.[19] Such was Mark's literary world.

To write this gospel story Mark would have had to survey his world to discern what form of the written word would be best received by his generally semi-literate audience. He could come up with a new genre but not a new audience. Knowing that his Gospel would be read aloud, performed, so to speak, in one sitting, he would have needed to find a format that easily crossed over from the oral tradition, a form that was both familiar and acceptable to his audience. The two most influential examples would have been the works of Homer and the Greek tragedian playwrights. There really was little else. Gilbert G. Bilezikian summarizes the situation as follows:

> On the basis of the evidence, it can be safely stated that the enduring success of Greek tragedy in the Roman world, including the city of Rome, was such that a person sufficiently conversant with cultural endeavors to undertake a project like writing the Gospel of Mark would have had at least a general acquaintance with it, such as was accessible to the common man, especially if he was literate in Greek—as Mark was.[20]

Bilezikian's work, considered the principal systematic analysis of the subject, draws a distinct line between the traditional Greek play and Mark's Gospel.[21] Theodore Weeden also affirms the Greek tragedy motif of Mark's Gospel, actually weaving much of his interpretation of Mark around that pattern.[22] Similarly, Dennis R. MacDonald offers an insightful examination of the Homeric motif in the Gospel of Mark.[23] Although dramatic Greek tragedian style permeates Old and New Testament writing alike, it is most pronounced and studied in Mark.[24]

What is essential to understanding the Greco-Roman literary influence is not the style but the philosophy that gave life to that style.[25] The

19. Bilezikian, *The Liberated Gospel*, 17.

20. Bilezikian, *The Liberated Gospel*, 38.

21. Smith, S., *A Divine Tragedy*, 209.

22. Weeden, *Mark: Traditions*, 1–168.

23. MacDonald, *The Homeric Epics*, 1–255.

24. Smith, S., "A Divine Tragedy," 209.

25. Aristotle's *Poetics* became the defining resource for critiquing Greek plays (Smith, S., "A Divine Tragedy," 209–210). Although not a play, Mark's narrative fits this Aristotelian definition.

Homeric epics and Greek tragedies revolve around a righteous hero who suffers and most often dies to appease a displeased deity. The martyr's death brings to the fore some ethical good that is then recognized and carried forward by his or her followers. The hero's reward for his or her suffering and noble unwavering-unto-death loyalty to the cause is immortality, either as eternal fame or a divinely granted post-mortem reward of some kind. Such eternal bliss would be found in the Elysian Fields (Perseus, Heracles), on Mount Olympus (Heracles),[26] or in Heaven (Moses, Elijah, Enoch). This philosophy permeated Jewish writing. It can be found in some of the sapiential writings, for example, the Wisdom of Solomon (Book of Wisdom) and in the books of 1–4 Maccabees. These texts will be examined in more detail in the next chapter so that we may better understand the influence of the Greek hero/martyr theme not only in pre-Markan Jewish literature but also in Mark. Mark's Jesus as the suffering servant (Isa 42, 50, 52, 53), the vicarious expiatory[27] martyr, fits this motif. Paul hints at this concept of Jesus in Romans 3–24-26:

> They are now justified by his grace as a gift, through the redemp-
> tion that is in Christ Jesus, whom God put forward as a sacrifice
> of atonement by his blood, effective through faith. He did this
> to show his righteousness, because in his divine forbearance he
> had passed over the sins previously committed. It was to prove
> at the present time that he himself is righteous and that he justi-
> fies the one who has faith in Jesus.

In this context, the story of the historic Jesus is that of the innocent, righteous, tortured, executed, acclaimed-only-after-his-death, believed-to-have-gained-some-divine-reward martyr whose sacrifice yielded a greater theological good.

---

26. The half-man nature of Heracles afforded an after-life in the Elysian fields, whereas his half-god nature was allowed enthronement on Mt. Olympus.

27 As used here and ongoing, the term "vicarious expiatory" refers to paying the price, suffering, for the sin of someone else.

5

Greeks, Martyrs, Maccabees, and Mark

The history of the consciousness of fault in Greece and in Israel will constantly be our central point of reference.

—Paul Ricouer, *Symbolism of Evil*

The Greek literary motif of the innocent suffering martyr, its portrayal in Psalms and Isaiah, in Maccabees, and the similarities in the Jesus-as-suffering-servant motif in Mark's Gospel is intrinsic to our discussion and worthy of a detailed look into that aspect of Mark's world. This will be beneficial when we examine his Gospel in more detail in later chapters. For now, however, we will turn our attention specifically to the most influential Greek philosophical and dramatic works and how the themes in those works trickled down through Jewish texts accumulating, most noticeably, in the books Maccabees 1–4 and eventually revealing themselves in the Gospel of Mark. This will give us an overview not only of how the centuries-old schema of sacrifice for the greater good was developed, expected, practiced, and assimilated into the Greek worldview, but also how it was subsequently assimilated into the Jewish worldview. This chapter will show that while Mark's theology is built upon the Jewish biblical tradition, his Gospel is built within the framework of the Greek worldview expressed in their great literary works. The combination of the powerful and profound Greek and

Jewish worldviews exhibited in their respective literature forms the foundation for defining the historic Jesus and places him, as well as Mark, within a certain historic context. Beyond that, however, we should not lose sight of the fact that out of the combination of Hebrew and Greek cultural motifs came Christianity's message of salvation.[1]

WHY?

Regardless of their diverse perceptions of the Jesus event, all the fledgling Christian communities were united in their common bewilderment of one particular issue—the inexplicable fact that their leader, whom they considered divinely anointed, was ignominiously executed as a seditious criminal. Gods could neither suffer nor die. Jesus' humiliating death was a fact that needed justification if he was to be found worthy of worship.

The crucifixion, the most contemptuous form of execution, was too scandalous to be ignored no matter how much the kerygma was proclaimed. The primitive church sought explanation for the crucifixion in Psalms and Isaiah, but that did little to allay orthodox Jewish concerns because, in their view, there was no getting around the Old Testament condemning interpretation of the crucifixion based on Deuteronomy 21:22–23: "When someone is convicted of a crime punishable by death and is executed, and you hang him on a tree . . . anyone hung on a tree is under God's curse." Jesus was convicted of sedition, a crime punishable by death, and hanged from a cross hewn from trees. As regards Mark 15:27, different translations offer differing labels for the two others crucified with him. The NRSV version refers to them as "bandits"; the KJV and Douay-Rheims versions calls them "thieves"; NIV uses "robbers."[2] The KJV and Douay-Rheims add verse 28 (missing in NRSV and NIV) telling us that Jesus' crucifixion fulfilled Scripture: "And he was numbered with the transgressors" ("wicked" in Douay-Rheims). That verse is a direct copy of Isaiah 53:12 and is an obvious insertion to connect Jesus to the suffering-servant motif of Isaiah.

Jews and Gentiles alike had to ask, "How could a man cursed and ignominiously executed be the Messiah?" Paul attempted to clarify the apparent

---

1. Harakas, "Must God," 196.

2 The common interpretation of Scripture that the two others crucified with Jesus were common thieves is misleading. The Romans reserved crucifixion for capital offenses only, such as sedition, not for petty crimes. The original term, *lēstai*, normally translates as *bandits* or *brigands* but as used by the Romans for crucifixion purposes it meant *revolutionary* or *zealot* (Aslan, *Zealot*,156; Brandon, *The Trial of Jesus*, 34, 103). On that fateful day on Golgotha all, including Jesus, were executed as *lēstai*, that is, revolutionaries.

contradiction by explaining that in order to remove the curse of the law Christ had to become a curse hanged from a tree (Gal. 3:13). He further acknowledges the Christ-as-criminal conundrum in 1 Corinthians 1:22–23: "We proclaim Christ crucified a stumbling block to Jews and foolishness to Gentiles." As for being the Messiah now "raised" (Mark 16:6), well, there was still that schema-challenging cognitive conflict we noted earlier in John 12:34: "The crowd answered him, 'We have heard from the law that the Messiah remains forever. How can you say that the Son of Man will be lifted up?'" Additionally, the Sadducees did not believe in resurrection (Mark 12:18), so the idea of a resurrected-from-the-dead Messiah was dramatically contrary to their schema. As for the Gentiles, such Old Testament adages meant nothing. The obvious reality for them was the fact that this Jesus was executed for sedition against the empire—a common fate for rebels—and they would be viewing that fact against the backdrop of a recently failed rebellion in the homeland of this same Jesus. It is hard to imagine more difficult circumstances for Mark to explain away.

The Evangelists sought justification for Jesus' scandalous death in the Old Testament, especially Psalms and Isaiah.[3] The victim in Psalms 22 and 69 and Isaiah 53 is portrayed as innocent. The heavy reliance on relating the suffering-servant Jesus back to those scriptures was done to explain his innocence. Mark's Jewish audience may have easily grasped the relationship. The foundational theme of Mark's Gospel is that of the suffering servant.[4] In Jewish literature the suffering servant motif originates in Isaiah, and yet there is nothing in Isaiah that refers to a Messiah, suffering-servant or otherwise. The suffering servant in Isaiah, the one who bears the burden of punishment and ransom, is the nation of Israel (Isa 49:3), not an individual.[5] A suffering Messiah would have been totally alien to Jewish thinking. That being the case, we are left to ask, "Why this motif?"

When considering the *Sitz im Leben* of Mark we must also consider the *Sitz im Leben* of the primitive church. Both were victims of a nation suffering under imperial cruelty. Both were strongly influenced by Greco-Judeo traditions in which suffering was due to God's displeasure. While God can do no evil, he is the authority for what is evil, that is, sin, and he is the source

---

3. Marshall, "The Death," 13–14. Girard posits that the Gospel writers' attempts to relate Psalms to Jesus is so excessive that it brings their need to do so into question (Girard, *The Scapegoat*, 102).

4. Weeden, *Mark: Traditions*, 52.

5 That the Messiah is implied in Isaiah is controversial. Objectively we know two things: 1) Isaiah never mentions a Messiah, 2) It categorically states in 49:3 that the servant is Israel.

of punishment for wrongdoing.[6] But when there was no sin, why require punishment? Why did Jesus have to suffer? If Mark's chief purpose for writing his Gospel was to prove that Jesus was the Messiah, then he needed to take several steps to build his case, none more important or difficult than justifying the crucifixion. His Gospel would serve as an apologetic for what happened to this Jesus whom he portrayed not only as the Messiah but also as an innocent victim, a righteous martyr, a vicarious sacrifice, a ransom to God for expiation of some great wrongdoing—a savior of others! If he was divine or divinely appointed and innocent, why did God need to subject him to such a tortured and disgraceful fate? Mark found an answer in the Greco-Judeo literary tradition that would make sense to his first-century audience.

Suffering, Death, and Salvation

There are essential elements that fit the martyr motif, beginning with the need for a martyr. A theological explanation for the innocent martyr, Greek, Jew, or Christian, was relatively straightforward: God required someone to pay compensation for some sin, some transgression, against him (or her in the pagan pantheon). And while the punishing, suffering-unto-death of a righteous innocent victim motif might have worked in the past (as in Psalms and Isaiah), it was a theme unfit for the Messiah motif. The primitive church, therefore, had to rationally and convincingly incorporate Jesus' historical end, his crucifixion, into its kerygamatic proclamation. This martyr-as-savior concept was nothing new; it was already deeply rooted in Greek and Jewish literature and culture.

The Maccabees

Many Jewish texts bear the imprint of the Greek archetype of the martyr as portrayed through centuries of Greek literature from Homer to Plato to the dramatic tragedians. Nowhere is this more evident than in the four books that describe the exploits of the Maccabees.[7] In 167 BCE the clash between the Jewish and Hellenistic cultures erupted when Antiochus IV Epiphanes, the Seleucid king of Syria, and Jason, the High Priest, attempted to impose pagan Hellenistic practices and erase Jewish religious traditions. In 1 Maccabees we read:

6. Williams, *Jesus' Death*, 91.
7. "Maccabees" is derived from the Aramaic "Maqqaba" meaning *hammer*.

And the king sent documents carried by the hand of messengers to Ierousalem and the cities of Iouda for them to follow precepts foreign to the land and to withhold whole burnt offerings and sacrifice and libation from the holy precinct and to profane sabbaths and feasts and to defile holy precinct and holy ones, to build altars and sacred precincts and houses to idols and to sacrifice swine and common animals and to leave their sons uncircumcised, to make their souls abominable in every unclean and profane thing, so as to forget the law and to change all the statutes. And whoever would not abide by the command of the king would die (1:44–50 NETS).[8]

Antiochus and Jason's attempt to subdue the Jews was marked by vicious torture of those who refused to give up their strict adherence to the Law and accept the Greek pagan practices. Many Jews accepted the new laws but "There was such an extreme of hellenization and increase in the adoption of allophylisma [alien ways] because of the surpassing wickedness of Jason, who was impious and no true high priest" (2 Macc 4:13 NETS), that many others were forced into open rebellion. This revolt was led first by Mattathias and then carried on more forcefully and successfully by his son Judas Maccabeus (Judah Maccabees). The eventual success of the Maccabean revolt gave rise to the Hasmonian Empire, the purging of Hellenistic pagan practices, and re-dedication of the Temple to Yahweh. The Jewish holiday of Hanukkah marks that re-dedication. The Hasmonians ruled, to a greater or lesser extent, from 140 to 64 BCE, when they were defeated by the Romans led by Mark Antony and Octavian. The Romans eventually turned administration for the area over to Herod the Great.

The four Maccabean books recounting the particulars of the horrendous atrocities inflicted on these martyrs were written over time between 161 BCE to 70 CE. Some historical evidence indicates that 4 Maccabees was written mid-first century CE[9]—conceivably concurrent with Mark. How much Mark used any of the Maccabean books is unknown. We should, however, recognize that the entwining of Greek and Hebraic concepts of God's requirement for a sacrificial suffering martyr influenced his beliefs. This schema defined its cultural worldview. While each Maccabean book

---

8. NETS (A New English Translation of the Septuagint). All four books are included in the Septuagint Bible (LXX). Only Books 1 and 2 are part of the Catholic Canon and Vulgate Bible; none of these books are included in the Protestant Canon. Other books related to the Maccabean revolt include Daniel and the Assumption of Moses. 2 Maccabees 2:24 identifies its author as Jason of Cyrene; authors of the other books are unknown.

9. Collins, "Finding Meaning," 179.

recounts the events of that time from a slightly different perspective, each, nonetheless, stays true to the theme of saving-martyrdom. The prominent heroic martyrs of the four books of the Maccabees are Eleazar(os), priest and philosopher; and a mother and her seven sons, all of whom are hideously tortured and executed for refusing to surrender to Antiochus's demands, in particular that they eat pig meat—an apostasy of the worst kind under the Law of Moses.

For many first-century Christians the archetype of the suffering innocent martyr in Greek literature was Socrates.[10] His strength of character, his stoicism, his righteousness, his peaceful acceptance of his fate combined with his intellectual challenge to his accusers, his unyielding commitment to his cause and refusal to compromise his principals to save his life all led to his continuing influence on how a true martyr should sacrifice himself. Socrates was put to death in 399 BCE, and the events portrayed in Maccabees begin ca. 167 BCE. The intervening years offer considerable time for the Socrates-as-martyr schema to become well rooted in both Hellenist and Jewish worldviews. This is evident in the remarkable similarities in speech, attitude, and behavior found in how Socrates and the martyrs in Maccabees accept the reality of their impending executions. There are common attributes to be found in the character of all these martyrs. First, they meet their fate with a calm dignity and resolve; second, they remain true to the end to their beliefs, principles, and faith; third, they staunchly believe in the righteousness of their actions; fourth, they firmly believe that certain wonderful rewards await them whereas punishing retribution await their executioners. Ironically, both the rewards and the retribution will be administered by the same God who, some might say "capriciously," requires their sacrificial deaths.

The motives behind the charges against Socrates and Eleazar, both aged philosophers, are based on religious and political concerns. Socrates, at age 70, is accused of impiety toward the gods and corrupting the youth of Athens. Eleazar, at 90, is indicted for his refusal to renounce his Jewish religious traditions and accept the pagan practices being imposed by Antiochus Epiphanes. Both men are concerned for the example their actions will set for the youth of their society and both reject offers and inducements to compromise their values in order to avoid execution. In 2 Maccabees Eleazar says:

> Even if for the present I would avoid the punishment of mortals, yet whether I live or die I shall not escape the hands of the Almighty. Therefore, by bravely giving up my life now, I will show

10. Bakker, "Beyond the Measure," 391.

myself worthy of my old age and leave to the young a noble example of how to die a good death willingly and nobly for the revered and holy laws (6:26–28).

Socrates encountered similar inducements to compromise his values in order to escape death. In the *Apology*, Plato's eloquent account of Socrates's speech at his trial, Socrates declares:

Men of Athens, I honor and love you; but I shall obey God rather than you . . . For know that this is the command of God; and I believe that no greater good has ever happened in the state than my service to God. For I do nothing but go about persuading you all, old and young alike, not to take thought of your persons or your properties, but first and chiefly to care about the greatest improvement of the soul (29).[11]

A common characteristic of the righteous innocent martyrs was their resolute confidence in God's retribution against their executioners. In 2 Maccabees when the sixth brother was about to die he warns: "Do not deceive yourself in vain. For we suffer these things on our own account, because of our sins against God.[12] Therefore astounding things have happened. But do not think you will go unpunished, for having tried to fight against God" (2 Macc 7:18–19). The other brothers and mother gave similar warnings before their execution (7:10, 14, 23, 28–29), culminating in the youngest brother's admonition, "But you, who have contrived all sorts of evil against the Hebrews, will certainly not escape the hands of God" (7:31). In the *Apology* Socrates offers an analogous admonition: "I would have you know, that if you kill such an [sic] one as I am, you will injure yourselves more than you injure me . . . For . . . the evil of unjustly taking away the life of another—is greater far" (30).[13]

As noted earlier, in the worldview of the time it was assumed that the suffering innocent martyr would reap rewards of some kind, be it fame, material possessions, or, most assuredly, resurrection into blessed eternal life with God. In Socrates's death scene as described in the *Phaedo*, Socrates says, "When I have drunk the poison I shall no longer be with you, but shall have taken my departure to some happy land of the blest."[14] In 2 Maccabees 7:9, when the second brother is brought forth to be put to death, he

---

11. Plato, *Apology*, 109.

12 Note the recognition and acceptance that their fate is due to God punishing them for their sins.

13. Plato, *Apology*, 109.

14. Plato, *Phaedo*, (115d).

exclaims, "You accursed wretch, you dismiss us from this present life, but the King of the universe will raise us up to an everlasting renewal of life, because we have died for his laws." And the mother of these brave mutilated martyrs, on seeing them tortured and killed before her eyes, encourages them by saying, "Therefore the Creator of the world, who shaped the origin of man and devised the origin of all things, will in his mercy give life and breath back to you, again, since you now forget yourselves for the sake of his laws" (2 Macc 7:23).

4 Maccabees

The book of 4 Maccabees offers much the same details as 2 Maccabees but takes on a deeper philosophical meaning. It describes the martyrs' same calm acceptance of their fate, and we see them giving similar reasons why they will not try to escape that fate (4 Macc 6:16–21; 27–30; 9:1–6); similar warnings of retribution (4 Macc 9:9, 9:32, 10:11, 10:21, 11:12); and proclamations of faith that their actions will result in their resurrection in eternal life (4 Macc 9:8, 16:25, 17:18, 18:3, 18:23). What is different in 4 Maccabees is its philosophical perspective, a perspective that reflects Aristotelian ethics. This book opens with:

> Since I am about to discuss an eminently philosophical subject—whether pious reason is absolute master of the passions—I would duly advise you to attend diligently to the philosophy here set forth. For the subject is essential to the path to knowledge for everyone and, furthermore, embraces praise of the greatest virtue: I speak, of course, of prudence (1:1–2).

The serious and purposeful study of ethics and moral behavior began with the ancient Greek philosophers. Aristotle's *Nicomachean Ethics,* arguably Western philosophy's finest examination of morality, is extensively devoted to an assessment of virtues and the character of the virtuous person. The virtues, such as temperance, courage, and prudence, are "praiseworthy dispositions," (1.13.1103a), and were central to the Greek understanding of moral goodness. In the *Ethics* Aristotle goes to great lengths to contrast virtue from passion, but the connection with Maccabees is his focus on prudence: "Moreover Prudence is intimately connected with Moral Virtue . . . and the right standard for the Moral Virtues is determined by Prudence."[15]

Aristotle's emphasis on virtue, passions, prudence, and reason is mirrored in the opening statement of 4 Maccabees. The choice between passion

---

15. Aristotle, *Ethics,* (10.8.1178a), 517.

and reason is a prime consideration in 4 Maccabees, and the author does not hesitate to point out that it is this choice every martyr must make:

> On the basis of many and diverse considerations I could show you that reason is absolute ruler of the passions, but I can demonstrate it much better from the bravery of those who died for the sake of virtue: Eleazaros, the seven brothers and their mother. All of these, in despising sufferings to the point of death, showed that reason has full control over the passions (1:7–9).

There is no doubt that their virtue not only made them praiseworthy but also renders them virtuous persons who, in the end, perform their function well, and that function was to save their nation by suffering and dying to placate an offended God.

In addition to those characteristics of the martyr revealed so far, 4 Maccabees emphasizes one other—*endurance*.[16] The following two verses are prime examples, the last of which emphasizes not only endurance and virtue but also the martyrs' assured belief in their resurrection into everlasting life with God.

> Having won, by their courage and endurance, the admiration not merely of all people but even of their abusers, they became the means by which the tyranny exercised against our nation was overthrown. They conquered the tyrant by their endurance so that through them our homeland was purified (1:11). For we, through the suffering and endurance shall gain the prizes accorded virtue and shall be with God, for whose sake we suffer (9:8).

An early recognition of the concept of atonement as ransom can be found in these Maccabean books. We are informed in 2 Maccabees 12:45 that after one battle Judas Maccabees learned that his fallen troops had been secretly wearing forbidden pagan tokens. He then took up a collection for them and sent it to Hierosolyma (Jerusalem) to provide a sin offering: "Therefore he made atonement for the dead so that they might be delivered from their sin." There are two passages in 4 Maccabees that are of particular interest in this regard because they, too, are early examples of atonement as ransom. The first is Eleazar's dying prayer at 6:28–29: "Be merciful to your people, and be satisfied with our punishment on their behalf. Make my blood their purification, and take my life in exchange for theirs." The second occurs in 17:20–22:

16. Williams, *Jesus' Death*, 166. Also, see Mack, *A Myth*, 107. Paul recognizes the connection between suffering and endurance in Romans 5:3–4: "But we also boast in our sufferings, knowing that suffering produces endurance, and endurance produces character, and character produces hope."

And these who have been divinely sanctified are honored not only with this honor, but also in that, thanks to them, our enemies did not prevail over our nation; the tyrant was punished, and the homeland was purified, since they became, as it were, a ransom for the sin of the nation. And through the blood of those pious people and the propitiatory of their death, divine Providence preserved Israel, though before it had been afflicted.

The four Maccabean books in general, and 4 Maccabees in particular, are dramatic evidence of a shift in Jewish thinking. Henceforth martyrs were to be recognized as having borne the burden of divine anger meted out because of the sin of a nation.[17] The Jesus communities and the Christ cult could have found an example for the saving aspect of the crucifixion—a blood ransom event wherein the martyr's sacrifice, his enduring suffering and death, paid off the debt of sin owed to God by the nation at large. This motif meshed well with the Jewish traditional understanding of their relationship with God. It also established a precedent for the future Christian explanation for Jesus' death as a ransom to atone for the sins of humankind.

Another source of the martyr-reward motif can be found in the deuterocanonical Book of Wisdom, also known as the Book of the Wisdom of Solomon. This book, absent from both the Jewish and Protestant canon, is included in the Catholic canon, the Septuagint, and the Protestant Apocrypha. It was written sometime in the first century BCE, supposedly in Alexandria, where Mark is reported to have spent his early missionary years. Solomon's name is attached to the title not because he had anything to do with its writing but because it deals with wisdom and virtue, two of his most notable characteristics. This book would have been known to a first-century Jewish and Hellenist audience and certainly available to Mark. It emphasizes not only eternal reward for those who suffer injustice while remaining righteously committed to obeying God's Law but also offers Mark a model for what befell Jesus.

Chapter 2 of the Book of Wisdom (NETS) looks at the world through the eyes of the wicked, who "were led astray, for their wickedness blinded them, and they did not know divine mysteries nor hoped for the wages of holiness nor recognized the reward for blameless souls." These ungodly ones contrive to "lie in wait for the righteous man, because he is inconvenient to us, and he opposes our actions and reproaches us for sins against the law and ascribes to us sins against our training (vv. 12–13). Such a one "is a burden to us even to see, because his life is unlike that of others and his behavior is different" (v. 15). And most foreboding of all:

17. Marshall, *The Death*, 15.

If the righteous man is a divine son, he will help him and will rescue him from the hand of those who oppose him. Let us afflict him with insult and torture, that we may learn how reasonable he is and may put his forbearance to the test. Let us condemn him to a shameful death, for, according to his words, he will be watched over (vv. 18–20).

Chapters 3, 4, and 5 of the Book of Wisdom assure us of the everlasting redemption for the just: "But the souls of the righteous are in the hand of God, and no torment will ever touch them" (3:1). Unlike where they fell victim to the wicked transgressions of others wielding earthly power, in death, " They will judge nations and rule over peoples" (3:8). And in the end, "they [be] counted amongst divine sons" (5:5). In addition to the canonical books of Isaiah and Psalms, the Book of Wisdom provided Mark with another source within which to contextualize the Jesus narrative, to justify Jesus' humiliating death. As will be shown in chapter 8, certain themes prominent in both the four Maccabean books and the Book of Wisdom are markedly reflected in Mark's Passion Narrative.

The Martyr in Greek Drama

Several Greek dramas contribute a considerable amount of narrative concerning the innocent martyr-as-savior theme. Sam Williams's remarkable study highlights several of these plays that portray, albeit in different ways, the honorable innocent martyr.[18] I would like to expound on the motif in three of those plays that portray the honorable innocent martyr. They are *Prometheus Bound* by Aeschylus, written ca. 500 to 400 years BCE; *Iphigenia in Aulis*, written by Euripides, ca. 400 years BCE; and *Antigone*, written by Sophocles ca. 500 BCE. We would do well to review them here with an eye toward their serving as a literary motif for Mark.

Prometheus Bound is the story of the Titan Prometheus, who opposes Zeus's desire to destroy humankind and start a new race of people. But Prometheus so loves humans that he thwarts Zeus's scheme by giving them the gift of fire. With fire all things are possible, allowing humans to achieve mastery and understanding of the world around them. They become more self-sufficient and less dependent on the gods. Prometheus's action not only spoils Zeus's plan but also diminishes Zeus's power. For this the angry supreme god punishes Prometheus by chaining him to a rock and having an eagle nibble on his liver daily. But Prometheus unrepentantly and *willingly*

---

18. Williams, *Jesus' Death,* 146–61.

endures his punishment because his love for humankind outweighs his self interest as a god.

> And none but I was found to cross his [Zeus's] will.
> I dared it, I alone; I rescued men
> From crushing ruin and th' abyss of hell—
> Therefore am I constrained in chastisement
> Grievous to bear and piteous to behold,—
> Yea, firm to feel compassion for mankind,
> Myself was held unworthy of the same—
> Ay, beyond pity am I ranged and ruled
> To sufferance—a sight that shames his sway![19]

Prometheus not only saved humankind from going to hell but also gave it life renewed, a life in which they could achieve fulfillment.

In *Iphigenia at Aulis*, written by Euripides, we find the cause of suffering comes from a whim of the goddess Artemis. On its way to attack Troy, unfavorable winds immobilize the Greek fleet at Aulis. To have favorable winds restored, the goddess Artemis, daughter of Zeus, sister to Apollo, demands the sacrifice of Agamemnon's eldest daughter, Iphigenia. Iphigenia accepts her fate willingly and rationalizes her self-sacrifice: "I can win all these good things by dying. Because of me Greece will be free and I will be famous." Here, too, we have evidence not only of the commonly held martyr's expectation of fame that is her due as a martyr but also recognition that she gives her life so that others might live. Two passages in particular found in *Iphigenia at Aulis* will resonate with Christians. To her father she says, "I can offer my body, which my mother bore, as the garland of a worshipper twined around your knees"; to her mother she says, "With the blood of my sacrifice I will cleanse the fateful curse."[20] With her body and her blood this maiden offers herself as a propitiatory offering and is willing to sacrifice her life so that her nation can be freed from the wrath of a displeased divinity.

Antigone, perhaps the most complex of the three plays, adds a decidedly religious conflict to the plight of the martyr. In the play, Thebes is attacked by forces led by Polynices, who is slain in battle. His adversary, King Creon, orders Polynices's body be left in the open to rot. Anyone defying his order is to be stoned to death by the citizens of the city. Antigone, Creon's niece, defies his order and attempts to bury Polynices. When Creon discovers what she has done, he orders her execution. Antigone argues that to leave the body unburied is against the law of the gods. Creon's son agrees with her, earning him Creon's wrath. Creon, however, bends a little, and amends his

19. Aeschylus. "Prometheus Bound," 176.
20. Euripides. "Iphigenia in Aulis."

execution order—instead of being stoned Antigone is to be buried alive in a sealed tomb. Before this happens, Creon is warned by a prophet that the gods are not pleased with his decision not to bury Polynices; therefore, he reverses all his orders. Tragically, Antigone, rather than suffer her fate in the sealed tomb, hangs herself before she gets news of her freedom. Although her death is not divinely ordained, it is a redemptive sacrifice nonetheless, as the Chorus reminds her "But in this ordeal thou art paying, haply, for thy father's [Oedipus's] sin."[21] They further assure her that through her pious loyalty to the gods she will achieve everlasting fame: "But 'tis great renown for a woman who hath perished that she should have shared the doom of the godlike, in her life, and afterward in death" (836). Not so different from the martyrs in Maccabees, Antigone is willing to die for her religious convictions rather than give in to the immoral order of a secular ruler.

The Acts of the Apostles 2:23–24 offers an explicit example of how Jesus fit the motif of the righteous martyr. In this passage Peter outlines what happened to Jesus, telling the Israelites that

> this man, handed over to you according to the definite plan and foreknowledge of God, you crucified and killed by the hands of those outside the law. But God raised him up, having freed him from death, because it was impossible for him to be held in its power.

We can diagram this passage according to the Greek/Maccabean martyr motif.

"this man, handed over to you according to the definite plan and foreknowledge of God	*God not only required this sacrifice but also set in motion the subsequent events,*
you crucified and killed	*the victim was tortured and put to death,*
by the hands of those outside the [religious] law	*appointed executioners (Creon, Antiochus, Pilate) who acted in opposition to God's law and yet fulfilled his plan,*
But God raised him up	*resurrection as compensation for suffering*
having freed him from death because it was impossible for him to be held in its power."	*the reward of eternal life.*

Table 2: Greek/Maccabean martyr motif diagram

21. Sophocles. "Antigone," 855.

Peter's explanation of Jesus' execution follows the Hellenistic under-standing of the righteous martyr's death as portrayed in both the Greek dra-mas and the Maccabean narratives. It is obvious that this motif persisted in Mark's Greco-Roman world. The incomprehensible death of the righteous could only be mandated by God; therefore, explanation for such death must come from God. So it made sense for the believers to turn to the Old Testa-ment, the only God-given source available to them, for an explanation for Jesus' death. And the best, albeit circumstantial, evidence to be found lies in Isaiah and Psalms. In reality, however, such justification was to be found elsewhere. It was to be found in the Greek archetype of an offended God who sets the stage, writes the plot, and directs the vindictive action. To avoid utter despair and to psychologically and culturally carry on, survivors ratio-nalize such tragedy by creating solace in the hoped-for rewards that await the suffering servant and the punishment of the perpetrators.

From a historic line of Greek dramas coursing subsequently through Maccabees we see the righteous innocent martyr suffering due to God's (or the gods') need for compensation for some transgression. To mitigate the divine wrath the martyrs endure suffering and go willingly to their death while steadfastly proclaiming to the end their righteousness and the righ-teousness of their cause. Through their humiliating death God is appeased and humanity, or at least a chosen part of it, is forgiven its transgressions. For their sacrifice the martyrs earn enduring fame, vindication, and exalta-tion through resurrection into eternal life with that same God (gods) who required their death. As for the executioners, their reward for playing their part in the divine plan is punishment, if not total destruction, and denial of life after death. This concept was born in Greek thought and portrayed throughout Greek literature. There is little doubt that this Hellenized motif is embedded especially in 4 Maccabees where propitiatory vicarious death and martyrdom as ransom is poignantly portrayed. The Maccabean litera-ture alone reveals the archetypical Jewish martyr accepting divine retribu-tion as ransom to atone for the sin of the nation.[22] Such a concept is not found in any other pre-Christian Orthodox Jewish literature.[23] It was, how-ever, a concept strongly embedded in the Greek worldview and portrayed in its literature, a concept readily available for the church to use to justify the scandal of the cross. It was a concept that was the very essence of Paul's theology. It was the concept by which the humiliation of the cross could be justified. Such justification would be pursued by the primitive church for years to come. Justin Martyr (ca. 100–65 CE), venerated saint, Christian

22. Marshall, *The Death*, 15.

23. Williams, *Jesus' Death*, 216.

apologist, and eventual martyr, writing in the second century CE, maintained the pursuit:

> But if any one objects that He was crucified, in this also He is on
> a par with those reputed sons of Jupiter of yours, who suffered
> as we have now enumerated. For their sufferings at death are
> recorded to have been not all alike, but diverse; so that not even
> by the peculiarity of His suffering does He seem to be inferior to
> them; but, on the contrary, as we promised in the preceding part
> of this discourse, we will now prove Him superior—or rather
> have already proved Him to be so—for the superior is revealed
> by His actions. [24]

As for Mark, his *theologia crucis* (theology of the cross) was becoming clearer. The followers of Jesus, emboldened by this martyr motif, were thus empowered to take up and carry on his cause symbolized by the cross.

24. Justin Martyr, *1 Apology*, 22.

PART III

According to Mark

6

Behind the Words

BEFORE EXPLORING SPECIFIC AREAS of Mark's Gospel it would be beneficial to look at it from a macro perspective. We will begin by examining what lies behind Mark's written words, that is, the historical context in which he wrote, his literary technique, how his gospel addressed the cultural and theological needs of the primitive church, and a review of some of Mark's most essential themes. What follows is a general survey of those features of Mark's Gospel that are important to understand his narrative in the context of his world. While some theological reflection may be exposed throughout this chapter, a more focused theological examination will be offered in chapter 9.

The Years Between

Prior to delving into Mark's narrative it is important to consider the years between the crucifixion and his writing, which I will refer to as the *interim*, as an entity in and of itself. This interim served as an interlude which allowed the many diverse Jesus groups to coalesce, to create their specific ideas and conclusions about the Jesus event, and to challenge anyone, even those within their own ranks, who held differing opinions. During this time the oft-repeated oral Jesus stories mutated from generalized recollections to theological purpose to fit the needs of those individual groups. From the crucifixion to the writing of Mark's Gospel there are no biographical literary resources available to inform us about Jesus. Mack shakes our complacent understanding of the Gospels with his conviction that Mark's Gospel is less the story of Jesus and more the story of the dynamics of primitive church development during those years.[1] Not unlike the surface features of our geographical world are shaped by subsurface tectonic frictional movements, what we see in the church texts of the first-century are the results of the friction between all the competing "heirs" to the legacy of Jesus. It is Cadbury's opinion that the final product that we call "gospel" is an amalgamation of all the various views, the compromises, the stories, and the materials created during the interim[2]—with a good bit of evangelistic creativity thrown in. Mark's narrative is a product of just one of the many Jesus factions vying to establish itself as the one true community of Jesus.

It was noted in the last chapter that the one thing the diverse groups who claimed Jesus as worthy of worship could agree upon was the need to explain the crucifixion. Other than general agreement about the basic events of the Passion Narrative, those groups were deeply at odds with one another. The Acts of the Apostles and Paul's epistles reveal the conflicts. The interim period served not only as a Petri dish that nurtured the growth of the divergent Jesus groups but also one in which their competing ideas were subjected to scrutiny, criticism, alteration, rejection, and assimilation resulting in, on occasion, alienation. In the end, the needs of the church were primary.[3] And those needs were determined by the church faction strong enough to survive the cultural, political, religious, and military turmoil, both internal and external, to the church itself. It is safe to conclude that Mark's narrative about Jesus advanced and asserted the beliefs of but one side of the primitive church, perhaps more than about Jesus himself.

Mark is Mark

The majority of Christians have read the Gospels and heard them quoted so many times that the details in each Gospel inevitably blend into one unified whole story, causing the individuality of each of the gospels to become lost. When we read the Gospels vertically, that is Luke beginning to end, Mark beginning to end, etc., it makes it difficult to recognize the various discrepancies between them. When read horizontally, however, that is, the same pericope or parable is read first in one Gospel and then in another and so on, we see very distinctive discrepancies. And this is certainly true

1. Mack, "The Innocent Transgressor," 155.

2. Cadbury, "Between Jesus," 82.

3. Cadbury, "Between Jesus," 82.

when comparing Mark to the other Gospels. Although Mark's Greek has been criticized as being very basic and lacking the fluency of Matthew's and Luke's, it is within that simplicity, compactness, and vigor of writing that one finds a sense of sincerity and realism in his rendition of the Jesus story. Mark is more direct in his narrative than the other Evangelists. Although Mark embellished and created parts of his narrative, the other Evangelists inflated their stories even more so. Some of the things they added include the long introduction regarding Jesus' lineage, the nativity events, details of Satan's temptation of Jesus in the desert, more parables, and the post-resurrection sightings and interactions between Jesus and the disciples. Our conundrum is this: Did Mark assume that his audience would know from tradition the details of some of his omissions and so he did not feel the need to report those details? Or, did he not include them because they did not happen, and the other Evangelists made them up to construct a theological framework that would validate Jesus' incarnate divinity while simultaneously providing a rationale for his brutal execution? It is easy to find advocates on both sides of the argument. We can either read a whole lot into what Mark wrote, allowing our schematic needs to fill in the blanks, or we can simply read Mark as it is—uniquely Mark; that is, what you read is what he meant to say, no more and no less. Prominent Markan scholars caution Mark can only be accurately understood free of influential bias from the other Gospels[4] and not to add conclusions that Mark himself does not make.[5] Although Mark drew from nearly forty years of tradition he was not simply echoing traditional narratives but creating a narrative for his late first-century audience.

General Structure and Observations

Recalling what the Apostolic Father Papias said about Mark, that he "wrote down accurately everything that he remembered, without however recording in order what was either said or done by Christ," implies that this Gospel is not an orderly, chronological presentation of the life and work of Jesus. This leads us to ask: How did Papias know that Mark did not record everything in order? We have become so familiar with Mark's Gospel that we take the accuracy of what he wrote for granted. Papias, writing at the beginning of the second century, would have been much more knowledgeable of the Jesus story and must have recognized the disorder in Mark's narrative.

4. Weeden, *Mark: Traditions,* 54.
5. Wrede, *The Messianic Secret,* 132.

Organization

Was there a comprehensive pre-Markan narrative that did put Jesus' ministry and work in chronological order? There is some speculation that there was an earlier gospel, an *Ur-gospel*, or *Ur-Markus*, that formed the basis for Mark, but there is no hard evidence that such a document existed. Regardless, something in Mark's narrative alerted Papias to recognize that it was not an orderly account. Perhaps he knew of something from the numerous individual accounts of Jesus' life circulating among the Christian communities that differed from Mark's account. Or, perhaps there were challenges to Mark's Gospel that were known to Papias but unknown to us today. We will never know for certain.

Papias' statement does alert us to some problems with this Gospel. An analytical reading of Mark reveals many of its flaws. There is disorder to it; for example, repetitions (two stories about the feeding of the multitude, similar clashes with the unclean spirits), and interruptions in dialog.[6] Despite these literary flaws Mark still manages to set the stage for the Passion Narrative. Nothing of Jesus' ministry is misrepresented and we can feel confident that, as Papias concluded, "Mark wrote down accurately all that he remembered." Of course, we do not know what Mark remembered or forgot. And by "accurate," we must realize that Mark was attempting to achieve neither chronological nor historical accuracy. His intent was to convince his audience of the messianic nature of Jesus. While we may in this sense accept Mark's accuracy, we are still left with a troubling concern: If Mark was Peter's interpreter they must have spent much time together. If so, then Peter did not reveal very much about Jesus, if this short, fractured narrative is all we have of the earthly life, including an intense three-year ministry, of the Messiah. Either Peter did not remember much or chose not to tell Mark all that he knew; or Mark did not remember all that Peter told him. Most likely, Mark was not an associate of Peter and he merely pieced together the accumulated stories of Jesus' life and death that circulated within the Christian community during the previous thirty to forty years. Whether he knew Peter or not, the Gospel of Mark is a collection of all those various Jesus stories that he (and perhaps others) pieced together to tell the story of whom they believed Jesus to be. We must accept that we will never resolve these issues and take Mark's narrative solely as is. If Mark's purpose was simply to present Jesus as the Messiah then organization and historical accuracy are not critical to achieving his purpose. Regrettably, however, it still seems that we are missing much of a remarkable life story.

6. Guy, *The Origin*, 21–35. It should be noted that repeated events may have happened more than once or, if not, the author repeated them to emphasize a point.

Literary Style and Devices

Mark's Gospel gains so much more life and meaning if we are aware of his style and the literary devices he used. His style and technique were shaped by the Greco-Roman literary world, the only one with which he would have been familiar. At the same time it is unique and he does incorporate his own creative methods into his composition.

Relation to Greek Drama

Mark's audience, Jewish and Gentile alike, would have been familiar with traditional Greek stories and would have easily recognized and related to the common imagery and motifs in Mark's Gospel. In chapter 4 we reviewed the extensive Greek literary legacy that shaped Mark's world. Here I want to review its dramatic characteristics. Although Mark's Gospel is a genre unique unto itself, it still reveals pervasive Greek literary influences. Several scholars have recognized this feature.[7] It is in Aristotle's *Poetics*, however, that we find more definitive proof of how Mark followed the accepted format of a Greek tragedy. Aristotle's *Poetics* holds the following specific criteria as essential in any dramatic narrative: *complication, unraveling* (also called *denouement*), *reversal of intention, tragic incident,* and *recognition.* These criterion will be noted individually as we progress in our subsequent review of Mark's Gospel.

Dramatist Personae

Besides Jesus, other principal *dramatis personae* include the disciples, the crowd, and the enemies of Jesus. These characters are essential throughout the entire story because not only the action but also the evolving theological meaning within the Gospel moves forward based on the interplay between them. The Gospel swells with dramatic tension in direct proportion to these interactions, such as the growing antagonism between Jesus and his enemies. As early as 3:6 Mark tells us that the Pharisees and Herodians[8] conspired on "how to destroy him." That ominous detail, repeated at 11:18 and 14:1, is unknown to the characters in the story but starkly revealed to Mark's audience.

7. See chapter 4.

8. There is no clear definition, biblically or historically, of "Herodians." The term was not used before the first century CE and first appears in Mark (Meier, "The Historical Jesus," 740; Dawsey, *Peter's Last Sermon,* 71.)

Mark has the ever-present crowd perform many functions. First, not only is it the source for those in need of Jesus' miracles but it is also the agency by which the story of those miracles is spread through the community (Mark 3:8). Second, it, and by extension all future audiences, is the recipient of Jesus' teachings. Third, he uses the attitude of the crowd as a defining contrast with that of his disciples.[9] Finally, that Jesus avoided arrest for as long as he did may be attributed, in part, to the fact that the religious authorities feared the crowd (Mark 11:32; 12:12). Such protection, however, was not to last, because Mark utilizes the crowd's fickleness to turn its honorific hosannas into horrific howls for execution, thus playing an important role in fulfilling Jesus' prophecy. I see the crowd as a substitute for the Chorus commonly found in Greek plays. Aristotle regarded the chorus in Greek drama as part of the cast of characters participating in the action.[10] The crowd certainly fits that role in Mark, where he uses it to give us background information, for example at 1:27 and 3:20; as recipient of Jesus' miracles, as in the feeding of the multitude (6:38–44; 8:4–8); students of his teaching (4:1; 7:14); and to move the plot along to its tragic climax with their persistent demands to have Jesus crucified (15:8–15).

Jesus' enemies include the religious establishment: scribes, Pharisees, High Priest, Sanhedrin, Herodians; and, of course, the evil spirits that repeatedly confront him. Interestingly, the Romans, who authorize and carry out the crucifixion, are not presented as enemies. Jesus directed his criticisms and confrontations toward the religious establishment rather than the occupying Roman forces. This hostility between Jesus and his enemies, slowly building throughout the Gospel, creates dramatic tension. The reader anticipates that, sooner or later, the mounting hostility will lead to a fatal climax. There are other *personae*, of course, such as John the Baptist,[11] who are only briefly noted and who are significant, but for lesser reasons. Intentionally or not, Mark follows the prevailing Greek literary dramatic concept to create undeniable dramatic tension that ends in tragedy and triumph.

Seams

Some of the disorder in Mark, as well as the other Gospels, may be attributed to the Evangelists' attempts to make a comprehensive narrative out of the

9. Keck, "Mark 3:7–12," 343.

10. Aristotle, Poetics, 18.5.

11. Some scholars see the Gospels' portrayal of the Baptist not as historically accurate but as creations of the Evangelists and the early church for theological purposes. See Marxsen, *Mark the Evangelist*, 43, fn 46; Bultmann, *History*, 246–247.

many individual Jesus stories created and embellished during the interim. This resulted in their stitching the individual stories together using *seams.* Seams are verbal connectors, words or phrases, usually introductory in nature, that connect one event to the next so as to move the narrative along. Examples include Mark 1:40, "A leper came to him . . ." and 9:14, "When they came to the disciples . . ."[12] and, "and he said," and "verily I say unto you."[13] As much as fifteen per cent of Mark's Gospel consists of these purely Markan connectors.[14] The seams are crucial evidence, literary finger prints, so to speak, of each Evangelist's creative contribution to his final product.[15] Mark selected, then stitched together, these individual stories and, where he deemed appropriate, interjected among them sayings attributed to Jesus from traditional sources. Many of the grammatical problems in Mark's narrative are due to this stitching together of independent stories.[16] A comprehensive examination of Mark's Gospel reveals that it consists of the pre-existing independent stories, sayings of Jesus, Mark's edits, and the Passion Narrative all tied together by the Markan seams.

Intercalations

John Donahue has done extensive work in identifying not only Mark's use of but also his purpose for the use of intercalations, which he defines as the insertion of an autonomous pericope after the beginning of the subject narrative that breaks the flow of that narrative.[17] The anointing at 14:3–9 is one such example.[18] Bilezikian identifies another intercalation at 3:7–12.[19] Detection of these literary characteristics help scholars distinguish Mark's redaction work from tradition material.

Son of—

Mark variously attaches three different unique epithets to Jesus. They are: *Son of God* (1:1, 3:11); *Son of Man* (2:10, 28; 8:31, 38: 9:9, 12, 31; 10:33, 45;

12 Grobel, "Idiosyncracies," 408.

13. Cadbury, "Between Jesus," 88.

14. Grobel, "Idiosyncracies," 408.

15. Grobel, "Idiosyncracies," 410.

16. Bultmann, *History*, 344.

17. Donahue, *Are You the Christ?*, 58.

18. Donahue, *Are You the Christ?*, 58–59. See this source for other examples of intercalations.

19. Bilezikian, *The Liberated Gospel*, 68.

13:26; twice in 14:21, 14:41, 62); and *Son of David* (10:47, 48).[20] Although volumes have been written about these enigmatic appellations, no definitive answer as to what Mark meant with their use has been forthcoming. Since Mark did not use these titles to denote Jesus' divinity,[21] we must ask ourselves the following questions: What did these titles mean to his first audience? How did Mark intend for those titles to be interpreted? How does our modern interpretation differ from the answers to those first two questions? Given their traditional use and meaning of these terms, they do not support Mark's portrayal of Jesus as the Messiah. Because Mark gives us no indication of how he meant those titles to be interpreted, we are left with schema-filling suppositions as to what the *Son of—* titles really mean in his Gospel.

The *Son of God* title opens Mark's Gospel; it is emphasized at the baptism, the transfiguration, and again by the centurion at the crucifixion. Mark uses it creatively to impress an essential point of his Gospel. The meaning of *Son of God* seems to be self-evident in that it bestows a genetic divinity, that is, a divine equality upon the son. In Mark it does not signify pre-existing divinity. Today we interpret this as foundational for the unique concept of the incarnation, in which case it is another of those schema-filling processes that has only scant connection with the reality of Mark's world—a magic/myth-minded world permeated by metaphorical god-speak.[22] Paul admits to the prevailing recognition of multiple gods in 1 Corinthians 8:5, "as in fact there are many gods and many lords."

Son of God was an appellation with a long history of attachment not only to special persons, most often kings or rulers, but also to holy men. God himself says that the nation of Israel "is my firstborn son" (Exod 4:22–23). It was commonly accepted in Greco-Roman culture that certain men were descended from a god. Alexander the Great was thought to be a Son of Zeus. Octavian (Augustus) was recognized as a divine son of God, and Romulus and Remus, the founders of Rome, were believed to have been sired by the god Mars. Greek literature included dozens of progeny created from the union of a god with a human female, of whom Heracles (Hercules), Zeus' son, is probably the best known. To the pagan polytheists, the majority of Mark's world, Zeus was God.[23] Any reference to "Son of God" simply meant

20. He also uses *Son of the Most High* (5:7), uttered by a demon, and *Son of the Blessed One* (14:61), from the High Priest.

21. Blackburn, "Deus et Homo," 190; Ehrman, *How Jesus*, 124–128.

22. Dunn, *Did the First Christians*, 62–66.

23. The Romans used the name Jupiter for Zeus, but essentially they are the same supreme god.

a son of Zeus.[24] The issue was further conflated by the fact that during An-
tiochus's brutal attempt to Hellenize Judea many shrines dedicated to the
Jewish God were renamed for dedication to Zeus (2 Macc 6:1–2 NETS).
Similarly for the pagans the term "most high God" meant Zeus, not Yahweh.

In general, the first-century crowd was inclined to recognize none
other but Zeus as God. We see this in Acts 14:11–13 where, by their miracle
work, Barnabas and Paul are mistaken for Zeus and Hermes. Neither Mark's
Greek nor Roman audience would have found anything extraordinary in
hearing that Jesus was a Son of God. Divine offspring were not uncommon
in their world. Indeed, Justin Martyr recognized the commonality of "Son
of God" when he wrote:

> And when we say also that the Word, who is the first-birth of
> God, was produced without sexual union, and that He, Jesus
> Christ, our teacher, was crucified and died, and rose again, and
> ascended into heaven, we propound nothing different from
> what you believe regarding those whom you esteem sons of
> Jupiter. For you know how many sons your esteemed writers
> ascribe to Jupiter . . .
>
> Moreover, the Son of God called Jesus, even if only a man
> by ordinary generation, yet, on account of His wisdom, is wor-
> thy to be called the Son of God; for all writers call God the Fa-
> ther of men and gods. And if we assert that the Word of God
> was born of God in a peculiar manner, different from ordinary
> generation, let this, as said above, be no extraordinary thing to
> you, who say that Mercury is the angelic word of God.[25]

Although Mark's Jewish audience would infer a different meaning
upon hearing "Son of God" they, like the Greeks and Romans, would have
found nothing exceptional in its use. Being God's progeny was not an unusual concept in Jewish tradition. The title could be bestowed on the king
(Isa 9:6), angels, or even the people of Israel. It is written in Genesis 6:1
that the "sons of God" (angels) took human women as wives. In 2 Samuel
7:14, God pledges that to David's child "I will be a father to him, and he
shall be a son to me." The adoption language found in Psalm 2:7: "I will
tell of the decree of the Lord: He said to me, 'You are my son; today I have
begotten you,'" was often used to denote the unique relationship between
God and the king.[26] Mark's Jewish audience must have been perplexed to
hear the Roman centurion declare Jesus to be "God's Son" (Mark 15:39). The

24. Collins, "Mark and his Readers," 88.

25. Justin Martyr, *1 Apology*, 21–22.

26. *Jewish Study Bible*: Tanakh translation, 1285.

statement is ambiguous—which God?—and seems to be a Markan insertion used to advance his theology. A Roman soldier's culture was based on, indeed his life depended on, worshipping the pagan pantheon in which Zeus was supreme God. This was not an ordinary foot soldier but a centurion, a commander of troops, someone who must have consistently complied with all official Roman codes of conduct—including the required sacrifices to Zeus/Jupiter—to achieve that rank. How, then, could this dedicated pagan instantly dismiss his life-long religious culture and refer to Jesus as the Son of the Jewish God? And why would Mark's Jewish audience accept the word of a commander of brutal Roman occupational forces? In all likelihood, they would have dismissed his claim as a Roman reference to Zeus, a claim unsupported by Jewish theology and tradition. In the dramatic fervor of the passion events, however, Mark creatively inserts the centurion's proclamation to further impress upon his audience what has been asserted at the baptism and transfiguration.

The Son of Man, a redeemer coming at the end time, was a well established concept in traditional Jewish literature, leaving little doubt that it was used in the pre-Markan Christian tradition as well.[27] The term originates in Daniel 7:13, but not as a title, as later Christian tradition would apply to Jesus.[28] The definitive meaning of *Son of Man* is elusive because it is used in Scripture in differing contexts. When God repeatedly addresses Ezekiel (KJV) as "Son of Man" it simply meant *man* in the generic sense. This same appellation is used extensively in the apocryphal book of 1 Enoch.

At his trial before the high priest, Jesus initially responds affirmatively to being the Messiah, the "Son of the Blessed One," but quickly refers to the Son of Man, not self-referentially, but vaguely in the third person "coming with the clouds of heaven" (Mark 14:62); more as an apocalyptic allusion to Daniel 7:13: "I saw one like a human being (*Son of Man* in KJV) coming with the clouds of heaven." As noted in chapter 5, Daniel in part alludes to the plight of the Maccabees. Where Daniel 7:27 refers to "the people of the holy ones of the Most High," "the holy ones" is a reference to the Maccabean martyrs.[29] The suffering-servant martyr and all that implies (see chapter 5), a common theme in Maccabees and Daniel, supported by Isaiah and Psalms, continues in Mark. In that regard, we are left to consider whether or not the historical Jesus cloaked himself in the "Son of Man" mantle taken from Daniel, or if he ever even actually used it. Some scholars believe Mark selected it

---

27. Crossan, *Jesus: A Revolutionary Biography,* 49–51; Perrin, "The Son," 17

28. Gonzàlez, *A History,* 38, fn 19.

29. Perrin, "The Son," 20.

from tradition material and creatively used it to validate the kerygma.[30] The primitive Christian church obviously found that Daniel favorably fit their messianic apologetic. Not only did Daniel 7:13–14, where the "Ancient of Days" [God] gave to the Son of Man everlasting "dominion and glory and kingship" over all people, fit their messianic and eschatological needs, but Daniel 12:1–4 was also foundational to the belief that innocent believers who suffer and die for God will triumph over their oppressors through the reward of resurrection and life ever-after in heaven. It is conceivable that Mark used "Son of Man" to establish a relationship for Jesus back to Daniel and hence back to the Maccabean suffering-servant martyr motif.

Whereas an outright claim to be Son of God or Son of the Blessed One would have brought charges of blasphemy (see Mark 2:7, 14:61–64), the ambiguous meaning of and well-established use in Judaic tradition of "Son of Man" was politically, religiously, and legally safer for Jesus to use. That would explain why he used it often even in public. Using "Son of Man" self-referentially gave him veiled reference to being the Messiah without him having to claim that title directly.

The two *Son of David* references (10:47, 48), like the "Son of God" references, are said *of* Jesus, not by him. The Son of David is a further emphasis on Jesus as Messiah, since David set the archetype of messianic movements.[31] Therefore *Son of David* designated Jesus as continuing the Davidic line of messiahship referred to in 2 Samuel 7:14.

Essential Themes

There are a few intrinsic themes that flow through Mark that are rarely discussed in general considerations of his Gospel, and yet these themes are the very foundation of the story he tells.

The Messianic Secret

The *messianic secret* is a major and yet perplexing premise in Mark. This theme, extensively developed by William Wrede and well accepted by other scholars,[32] refers to the numerous instances in Mark where Jesus, while

30. Crossan, Jesus: *A Revolutionary Biography*, 50; Mack, *A Myth*, 278.

31. Horsley, "Popular Messianic Movements," 475.

32. Of Wrede's *The Messianic Secret*, Theodore Weeden Sr. writes, "The influence of Wrede on Markan interpretation has been staggering. Most explanations of the Gospel take for granted his basic insight." Weeden, *Mark Traditions*, 138. Dibelius, *From Tradition*, 223, agrees with Weeden's assessment.

trying to convince his disciples that he was the Messiah, took considerable effort to keep his messiahship secret from the public, despite performing messianic-like miracles in full glare of that public—the ubiquitous *crowd*. Simply stated, Jesus the Messiah was trying to hide in plain sight. Once recognized, this feature adds an unique depth of understanding of Mark's narrative by tying together various events and behaviors.

Our first hint of the *secret* comes early in the Gospel, in the baptism scene. Of this God-Jesus interface in his narrative, Mark limits the witness to this event to Jesus only: "He saw the heavens torn apart and the Spirit descended like a dove on him" (1:10). So, while Mark's audience is privy to what Jesus saw, those in the narrative are not; therefore, Jesus' secret remains intact even in this essential gospel event. Mark then quickly moves his audience deeper into the secret at 1:23–25, where Jesus has his first encounter with an "unclean spirit." This spirit greets Jesus with "What have you to do with us, Jesus of Nazareth? Have you come to destroy us? I know who you are, the Holy One of God." And Jesus responds with, "Be silent, and come out of him!" Here we might question if Jesus means for the spirit to be totally quiet, or if he means be quiet about his being the "Holy One of God." The question is answered in subsequent episodes with both spirits and humans alike. As regards the spirits, Mark develops a pattern of recognition by the spirit followed by Jesus' admonishment to be silent. At 1:34 we find that "he would not let the demons speak, because they knew him"; at 3:11–12; "Whenever the unclean spirits saw him, they fell down before him and shouted, 'You are the Son of God!' But he sternly ordered them not to make him known." In the well-known Gadarene Demoniac incident (5:2–20) the unclean spirits speaking through the demoniac again recognize Jesus as "Son of the Most High God." Jesus silences them forever by casting them into the swine herd that then plunges en masse into the sea.

Jesus' pattern of prohibiting disclosure of his miraculous works continues in his encounters with humans as well. After publicly healing the leper (1:40–43), Jesus tells him to show himself to the priest (in compliance with the Law), but to "say nothing to anyone." It occurs again at 5:35–42 where we find Jesus in front of a large crowd when it is announced that the daughter of Jairus, the leader of the synagogue, had died. Jesus orders everyone to remain there and takes Peter, James, and John and goes to Jairus's house, where they find a small weeping and wailing crowd. Jesus orders them to stay out and takes his three disciples and the mother and father to the girl's room where he revives her. Then he "strictly orders them that no one should know of this" (v. 43). Convinced that she was dead, the crowd of mourners would now see her alive, so it seems his order of silence would not have much effect. Similarly, at 7:36, Jesus, after healing the deaf man, ordered the witnessing crowd not to tell of his work, and yet, "the more he ordered them, the more zealously they proclaimed it." Again, after healing the blind man (8:26), Jesus tells him to go straight home (a private setting) and not to go into the village (a public setting); and yet in 10:51–52 he heals another blind man in front of a large crowd and gives no order for silence. Our final, and perhaps the most dramatic, piece of evidence of the messianic secret is to be found in the transfiguration event in 9:9. Immediately following the transfiguration he "orders" those who witnessed it, Peter, James and John, "to tell no one about what they had seen until after the Son of Man had arisen from the dead." All these episodes present a paradoxical relationship between Jesus' public displays of miracles followed by his prohibitions to keep those miracles secret. These contradictions are obvious in the Gospel, but Mark never explains them. The messianic secret just hangs there and we are left to speculate as to the mystery of the messianic secret.

While the messianic secret is an essential feature in Mark, the afore-mentioned episodes, their theme and their common dialogue, are so consistent and so formulaic that as historic fact they are suspicious. As theological apologetic, however, they further Mark's attempt to establish Jesus as the divine Messiah.[33] Mark does this by first portraying those other spiritual, albeit unclean, creatures, the demons, as instantly recognizing Jesus' spiritual nature. Second, Mark reinforces his narrative proof of Jesus as having divine powers by detailing his miraculous healing power. Third, he gives us the transfiguration episode, where Jesus is displayed in divine glory. Although the miracle events come with Jesus' prohibition against proclamations of his divine nature, they nonetheless present him as someone special. Very early in the Gospel (1:28), Mark writes, "At once his fame began to spread," and such fame would not restrain recognition that Jesus was extraordinary. As we study some of those miracle stories more fully, we cannot help but recognize a common feature, be it the leper, the deaf man, or the blind man—they all actively sought Jesus because of his fame as a miracle-worker. All this makes the messianic secret more incomprehensible and we wonder all the more, "Why attempt secrecy?"

Such divine secrecy would be a familiar theme to Mark's audience. The use of such secrecy was a common motif in Greek and Roman stories used to avoid detection of the divine person by humans and thus promote reverence.[34] Greek literature often includes instances where gods and demigods anonymously interact with humans. Second, it fits with Aristotle's emphasis on *recognition* in good dramas. In a well-written tragedy the pursuit of

---

33. Wrede, *The Messianic Secret*, 126.

34. Collins, "Mark and His Readers," 90.

recognition is, according to Aristotle, one of the most powerful elements driving the plot.[35] Since the identity of Jesus is a frequently-raised issue in Mark,[36] ultimate recognition is a decisive turning point in the story. This theme will be covered in more detail in the next chapter with the Jesus-Peter confrontation at Caesarea Philippi.

In first-century Judea, there were some rebellious brigands who assumed the mantle not only of king but also of being the "anointed one."[37] The Judaic concept held that the Messiah would be a human leader (see Micah 5:2), a traditional worldly ruler that would deliver Israel from its enemies. Mark's Jesus had to work around that schema, not by direct confrontation but by humble behavior, miracle work, teaching, prophecy, and allusions to his resurrection. Because of their different understanding of the nature of the Messiah, publicly proclaiming his messiahship too early would have been too great a distraction for disciples and crowd alike. They would have expected a political leader, not a spiritual savior. Additionally, his enemies could have used such a claim against him sooner than they did, thus abruptly ending his teaching and healing ministry.

Jesus As Teacher

Jesus as teacher is an essential theme in Mark. At 1:22 he writes, "He taught them as one having authority, and not as the scribes." Indeed, it was Jesus' teaching that became the overt threat to systemic Judaism and, thus, to the authorities who maintained control over the nation through their interpretive control of that religion.[38] This becomes obvious early in the Gospel (Mark 3:6) when, immediately after a teaching conflict regarding the Sabbath, the authorities decided that Jesus had to be destroyed. The threat continues on to 11:18 when the chief priests persisted in their plans to kill Jesus because "the whole crowd was spellbound by his teaching."

Mark frequently points out that his disciples received more extensive teaching in private: "He did not speak to them except in parables, but he explained everything in private to his disciples"(4:34).[39] Mark does not tell us what Jesus taught in private, but he does tell us that on a number of occasions (8:31–9:1, 9:31–10:1,10:32–45) Jesus taught his disciples about himself, his mission, his impending suffering, death and resurrection, true

---

35. Aristotle, *Poetics*, 6.5.

36. See Mark 1:27, 2:7, 3:22, 6:2, 6:14, 8:27, 11:28, 14:61, 15:2.

37. Horsley, "Popular Messianic Movements," 474.

38. Dodd, *The Founder*, 77.

39. See also Mark 7:17, 8:31–33, 9:2–9, 9:33–37, 10:10–11

discipleship, and the kingdom of God—and on each occasion his disciples failed to grasp his meaning.

Suffering and Discipleship

As Markan research developed, it was noted that Mark raises both a polemic against the disciples and portrays Jesus as a suffering servant.[40] In chapter 5 we examined the martyr aspect of the suffering servant theme and how it was well established in Greek and Jewish tradition. We revisit it here but now look at it in conjunction with Jesus' relationship with his disciples and discipleship in general. One of the most significant themes in Mark is discipleship.[41] And yet Mark's portrayal of the Twelve leaves us challenged to say anything positive about them. To be honest, they come across as dullards throughout the entire narrative. This raises at least two intriguing questions: If Mark was Peter's interpreter, why did Peter disclose such a damaging self-portrayal? If Eusebius was correct about Mark being accurate, then the disciples were as ignorant as Mark portrays them. Further, if Mark was attempting to bolster and sustain the Jesus movement in the Christian church, why attack the very men who were Jesus' closest confidants and pillars of the faith? Mark's portrayal of the character of the disciples is manifestly puzzling.

Mark goes beyond discipleship to focus on suffering-discipleship. There are three specific times where Mark juxtaposes Jesus' dramatic teaching about his impending suffering and death against the utter failure of the disciples to understand. The first of these occurs at 8:27–33, the famous Caesarea Philippi event. When at 8:31 Jesus informs the disciples that the Son of Man must "undergo great suffering . . . and be killed," Peter rebukes him, causing Jesus to rebuke Peter in return—"Get behind me Satan"—for failing to grasp the divine plan, which included suffering and humiliation. Jesus then calls the disciples and the crowd together and teaches them what true discipleship means. At 9:31 Jesus once more informs his disciples that the Son of Man is to be killed, and for a second time they fail to comprehend: "But they did not understand what he was saying and were afraid to ask him" (v. 33). Again, Jesus follows up with instruction on true discipleship (v. 35). Yet again, at 10:33 Jesus informs the disciples that the Son of Man will be tortured, condemned to death, and killed, prompting James and John to ask that he grant them a place of honor when he comes into his glory, and Jesus must again teach the meaning of true discipleship. At 6:52,

40. Weeden, "The Heresy," 10.
41. Vaage "Another Home," 741.

after the feeding of the five thousand, Mark sums up the character of the disciples: "They did not understand about the loaves [Jesus' miracle power], but their hearts were hardened." Jesus' exasperation seems to get the better of him in 9:19: "How much longer must I put up with you?" Imagine how he felt knowing that his hand-picked confidants would abandon him to suffer his terrible fate alone.

Traditional Christian dogma has masked Mark's portrayal of the disciples. It is not how we have come to know them through the Acts of the Apostles, other writings, through tradition, or by the accounts we have of their missionary work. William Wrede contends that Mark meant no disrespect of the disciples because their lack of understanding was a natural reaction to the situation and to the messianic secret; a valid supposition given their faithful post-resurrection behavior.[42] In chapter 9 we will examine one other reason for Mark's seemingly disrespectful portrayal of the apostles.

Other than the cursory recognition of Jesus as the Messiah by Peter, the disciples fail to grasp that this Messiah is a suffering Messiah. At Mark 10:45 Jesus says, "For the Son of Man came . . . to give his life as ransom for many"—this messiah came as a suffering servant, the vicarious martyr examined in chapter 5. Tying discipleship to suffering amounts to a demand for imitation, a prerequisite for admission into the kingdom of God. The origin of these themes—a suffering-servant martyr, resurrection, expiating atonement, resurrection by the same God who demanded a vicarious death, and the reward of everlasting life—are to be found in the Greek worldview and carried on in Jewish tradition.

Political Considerations

We cannot escape the reality that Mark was writing in a world politically, culturally, militarily, and religiously dominated by Rome. We have already reviewed the peril that existed for the Jewish and Christian communities during the turbulent years (66 to 70 CE) surrounding Mark's writing. Certainly neither Romans nor orthodox Jews would welcome anyone associated with a supposed Jewish Messiah, someone who seemed to have authoritarian ambitions. The Acts of the Apostles and various references in Paul's Epistles give us evidence that these new Jesus communities were undeniably at odds with the established Jewish religious authorities. Mark's Christianity stood in conflict to both Romans and Jews, the two most dominant cultures in his world. But it was Rome that was all-powerful. At the time of his writing

---

42. Wrede, *The Messianic Secret*, 105–106. Weeden (*Mark: Traditions*) has a much different theory which will be discussed in chapter 9.

Rome had either crushed or was about to crush the Jewish rebellion. Mark's eyes would see a world dominated by the invincible Romans who had just reduced Judea to near extinction. Mark, a Jew with roots in Judea, was (supposedly) living in the capital city of an empire at war against his homeland. He was a professed Christian—that blasphemous religious sect that not so long ago was blamed for burning down half of Rome and that worshipped, as king no less, a man who was executed for sedition against the empire. And just recently two prominent Christian leaders had been executed in the imperial capital. Nearing the end of the first century Roman rulers would have been understandably suspicious of all things related to rebellious Judea. Both for his survival and that of the Christian movement Mark could not risk offending the Romans by writing a story that implicated them in the execution of Christianity's professed Messiah. Politically and theologically it would be to Mark's advantage to blame the powerless and scattered Jews rather than alienate Rome. And he does so quite skillfully.

Mark portrays Jesus as one seeking religious rather than political reform. Indeed, all the Evangelists portray Jesus as standing in opposition and disapproval not of the Roman occupiers but of the established Jewish religious authorities. As early as chapter 2 Mark begins to build dramatic tension between Jesus and the Jewish authorities (2:6–8, 2:18–20, 2:24–28) and by 3:6 he reveals that the Pharisees and Herodians were plotting to destroy Jesus.

Separation from Judaism

In chapter 3 Mark begins the separation of Jesus (and thus Christianity) from the Jews. In 3:13–19, Mark gives us the story of Jesus choosing the Twelve. Of particular interest is 3:18 where Mark writes that one of the Twelve was Simon the *Kananaios*, Cananaean, which is Aramaic for *zealot* (Gk. *zēlōtēs*).[43] It was demonstrated earlier that Mark translated his infrequently used Aramaic expressions but here he chooses not to do so. *Kananaios* meant one who had uncompromising devotion to his religion. Its roots in first-century Judaism can be traced back to 2 Maccabees 4:2, where it is used to mark someone who was a "zealot for the [Jewish] laws," and 4 Maccabees 18:12 proclaims Phineas as a "zealot." Its association back to Maccabees suggests resistance to authority. By the time Mark wrote his

---

43. Most NT translations render that as Simon the *Canaanite* or *Cananean*. Luke, writing some 15 years after Mark, writes "Simon the Zealot" in Acts 1:13. The KJV translation uses *zealot*, but the writers of the KJV didn't have to worry about Roman sensibilities.

Gospel the term *zealot* had become politicized, an official label for those Jews in rebellion against Rome.[44] To the Romans "zealot" meant rebel. If the Romans heard the word "zealot" affixed to a follower of this Jesus who had been executed as a rebel they would immediately connect him and his associates with the warring rebels in Judea.

Mark continues to separate Jesus from his Jewish roots at 3:21, where his family tried to restrain him, and likewise in 3:31–35 where he awkwardly renounces his familial relationship with his mother and brothers by using a vague theological definition of family. Mark could have chosen any number of ways to make this theological point, but here he takes the opportunity to use this strange rejection of his immediate Jewish family and thus, by inference, separates Jesus from his collective Jewish family. In 6:1–4, Mark takes a different approach and instead has Jesus' hometown reject him. While the approach is different, the result is the same—Mark is cutting Jesus' ties with his Jewish roots. Mark may have had one other political motive for either creating or choosing stories that depicted a dissolution of Jesus' Jewish connections. It would have sent a subtle message of separation from the Jerusalem church, an indication, perhaps, that he favored the Hellenist Christ cult.

Roman Bias

Mark's portrayal of the Romans is more generous than his portrayal of the Jews. The first evidence of this is at 12:17, where the Pharisees and Herodians challenge Jesus about paying taxes to the emperor. Jesus' literal answer, "Give to the emperor the things that are the emperor's and to God the things that are God's," would apparently ease Roman fears of refusal to pay the emperor his due. But this raises a deeper challenge—does the tribute demanded from a conquered land, a land believed to be given by God to the conquered, really belong to the emperor? The Zealots would, of course, say no.[45]

Next, we have Mark's portrayal of Pilate's seeming reluctance to crucify Jesus (15:1–15). Historically, this is extremely unlikely. (This will be covered in review of the Passion Narrative in chapter 8.) Pontius Pilate was, perhaps, the cruelest of Roman Judean procurators—so much so that he was recalled to Rome[46]—and would not have hesitated to crucify a Jew claiming to be a "king." Jesus was, however, crucified, and there was no getting around the

44. *Zealots* as a recognized subversive political resistance group did not exist until the Jewish uprising of 66–70 CE (Horsley, "Popular Messianic Movements," 472).

45. Brandon, *The Trial of Jesus*, 66–68.

46. Josephus, *Antiquities*, 18:55–85; Aslan, *Zealot*, 149.

fact that only Roman officials could order his crucifixion. Here Mark avoids insulting Rome at the expense of historical fact. He portrays Pilate as being reluctant while the Jewish "chief priests stirred up the crowd" (15:11), demanding crucifixion.

Mark tells us the Jewish chief priests and scribes as well as those passing by ridicule Jesus for his inability to save himself, thus validating their opinion that he was neither God nor king (15:29–32). Now contrast those disdainful Jews with Mark's portrayal of the Roman centurion who stands guard at the cross and proclaims, "Truly this man was God's Son!" (15:39). According to Mark, the very first person to declare Jesus the Son of God was neither one of his disciples nor a Jew, but a Gentile. And not even an ordinary Gentile but a Roman soldier! Interestingly, the centurion recognizes Jesus as "God's Son," and not "King of the Jews" as the "inscription of the charge" read (15:26), thereby dissolving another of Jesus' Jewish connections. In summation, Mark would have us believe that the Jews were not only the primary perpetrators of Jesus' crucifixion and rejecters of his divinity but also that the Romans were reluctant participants and the first to recognize Jesus' divinity. None of this holds up to either historic scrutiny or logic but, considering the dangerous predicament the Christian community was in at the time, Mark deftly avoids ruffling Roman feathers.

Geography

Despite his chronological and historical inaccuracies, his awkward insertions, and his own creations, Mark still maintains a recognizable chronological-geographical direction.[47] Early in the Gospel Mark tells his audience that Jesus "came from Nazareth of Galilee" (1:9). His fame initially "spread throughout the surrounding region of Galilee" (1:28). Galilee and its well-known lake are not just prominent but also significant in Mark's narrative. Marxsen refers to Mark as the "Galilean Gospel."[48] Jesus begins and sustains the bulk of his ministry in Galilee, especially around Capernaum and the Sea of Galilee, moves inevitably toward his fate in Jerusalem, and after his death he directs his followers back to Galilee (16:7). Although the authorities in Galilee, which was under the control of Herod, who had executed John the Baptist, were getting increasingly annoyed with Jesus, he had maintained some level of safety there. It was only when he went to Jerusalem, which

47. Guy, *The Origin*, 36.

48. Marxsen, *Mark the Evangelist*, 66. An entire section of Marxsen's work, entitled "The Geographical Outline," offers a detailed analysis of Mark's use of geography.

was under much stricter Roman control, especially during Passover, that his fate was met.

It is possible that Mark had political/theological reasons for bringing the focus of his Gospel full circle back to Galilee. Consider that Mark would have factual knowledge of the flight of Christians out of war-torn Jerusalem to the temporarily safe environs of Galilee; therefore it made narrative sense to have the young man direct the women at the empty tomb to tell the disciples that Jesus will meet them in Galilee. Additionally, Mark skillfully sets the stage for the expected Parousia to take place there. The Parousia, the return of Jesus to rule God's Kingdom on earth, would prove he was the Messiah. Considering the collapse of the world around them, Mark's audience would have been easily receptive to his theological purpose. Harold Guy opines that Mark demonstrates a lack of knowledge of Palestinian geography.[49] If so, then either Mark was a native of Palestine and manipulated the geographical facts of his Gospel to fit his theological purpose, or he was not a native of Palestine and made the geographical errors out of ignorance. When all is taken into account, geography played an important role in Mark's narrative.

Theios Aner

Behind the entirety of Mark's Gospel lurks the haunting shadow of a common first-century figure known as the *theios aner*, that is, divine man. A *theios aner* was a Hellenistic concept referring to a supernatural philosopher divinely endowed with wisdom and miraculous powers. Many scholars consider it to have influenced Mark's theology as well as a motive for his writing his Gospel. The *theios aner* theory will be covered in detail in chapter 9.

49. Guy, *The Origin*, 150.

7

According to Mark

THUS FAR WE HAVE examined many of the political, historical, cultural, literary, and religious traditions, events, and experiences that filled Mark's world. In this chapter we will survey his Gospel with an eye toward demonstrating how those historical and cultural forces are reflected in his narrative. To keep this in perspective, Mark was writing a story about events that occurred about forty years earlier, events that initiated a religious movement at odds with the world around it. Attempting to promote and sustain that religious movement required him to fashion his narrative in such a way as to safely protect and advance a faith, not a historical record.

The Beginning

Before receiving its modern formal title, *The Gospel according to Mark*, this narrative was referred to as *Kata Markon*, "According to Mark."[1] When it was first introduced into the Jesus communities, however, it had neither a title nor an identified author.[2] So the first words Mark's earliest audience heard from the *Methurgeman* (lector) were: "The beginning of the good news [gospel = euangelion] of Jesus Christ, the Son of God" (1:1). Mark's story bursts open with this short incipit, wasting no time with a lengthy

1. "The Gospel According to Mark," in *The Holy Bible*, Thomas Nelson Bibles, (2003), 1077.

2. Ehrman, *How Jesus*, 90.

introduction, not even with a complete sentence. But with that simple well-loaded dramatic phrase Mark does three things: one is to use the term "gospel" in a novel manner;[3] another is to identify Jesus as the "Christ," that is, Messiah; finally Mark tells us that this "Gospel" is of Jesus Christ,[4] *the Son of God.* This introduction is unique. It is different from most Greek dramatic plays, for example, *Prometheus Bound* or *Medea,* which most often have a long prologue meant to give the audience enough background information to set the stage for the drama about to unfold. Brief though it is, it still meets the definition of a prologue given in Aristotle's "Poetics,"[5] which was to introduce the story to the audience in simple but dramatic fashion. Mark's opening certainly does that. Scholars do not agree on where Mark's prologue ends. Many scholars believe everything up to the Passion Narrative is prologue, while others end it at the baptism.[6] Regardless, Mark gets right into the Jesus story without any biographical backstory, no claim of pre-existent divinity, or of royal heritage. Those stories would have to await the writing of future Gospels, where Jesus' divinity and royal lineage needed to be established. Mark moves quickly into the introduction of Jesus' divine nature through his baptism.

The Baptism

Mark's presentation of the baptism event has led to a long-standing theological controversy. As written, Jesus' divinity began at his baptism, thus leading to the development of the *adoption theory.* What Mark *writes* is purely adoptionist: "And just as he was coming up out of the water, he saw the heavens torn apart and the Spirit descending like a dove on him. And a voice came from heaven, 'You are my Son, the Beloved; with you I am well pleased'" (1:10–11). We have previously observed how much Psalms influenced the Gospels' characterization of Jesus. His baptism narrative must be read in conjunction with Psalm 2:7–8: "I will tell of the decree of the Lord: He said to me, 'You are my son; today I have begotten you.'" Dibelius suggests that Mark was using the event to verify Jesus' pre-existing divinity.[7]

---

3. Marxsen, *Mark the Evangelist,* 124–127.

4. Some scholars consider Jesus himself to be the gospel (the good news) while others agree with the traditional recognition of the narrative being the gospel.

5. Aristotle, *Poetics,* 12.2.

6. Weeden, *Mark: Traditions,* 8–10.

7. Dibelius, *From Tradition,* 231, fn. 1; 272–274. This is Dibelius's personal assumption; he offers no evidence to support his claim.

Without any insinuation of incarnation anywhere in his Gospel, that is projecting a substantial premise into Mark that is just not there.

In our modern Christology the adoptionist view might be upsetting to some. In the Roman/Hellenist world of Mark, however, it not only made sense but had great significance. In Roman culture, an adopted son actually had higher status than a biological son. For example, history tells us very little about Julius Caesar's natural son (by Cleopatra) Caesarion, but much to say about his adopted son, Caesar Augustus, the first emperor of Rome. Augustus was Julius's nephew who Julius legally adopted, thus granting him all hereditary rights to wealth and power over those of Caesarion.[8] Mark's audience, Roman and Jewish, would have been more receptive of this adoptionist inference than the subsequent incarnation theory.

A close examination of the baptism story reveals some interesting facts. First, Mark does not tell the audience that Jesus is the incarnate Son of God; instead, he echoes Psalm 2:7–8—"today I have begotten you"—thus indicating Jesus' divinity began with the baptism. Second, only Jesus heard the voice. If this was a major pronouncement, why not report that all those in attendance heard it? While this might have been in keeping with the messianic secret there is no admonishment to maintain the secret. Third, Mark alludes to Roman and Jewish myths in 1:10, beginning with, "he saw the heavens torn apart." That phrase would have immediately caught the attention of Mark's Roman audience because the Romans often used a reference to the rending of the heavens as a portent of a momentous event.[9] Mark's Jewish audience would also have recognized the opening of the heavens as a sign of divine communication, as in Isaiah 64:1, "O that you would tear open the heavens and come down . . ."[10] Next Mark writes, "and the Spirit descending like a dove on him." We assume Mark meant the Spirit *of God*, but the Jewish religion did not use this shortcut. In Jewish use the word *spirit* without "of God" denotes either a demon spirit or wind.[11] In that vein, it was a common belief at the time that the divine Spirit like that which moved over the water at creation would infuse the Messiah.[12] A referential link may also be seen in Isaiah 42:1 where, after speaking of the servant as

8. Ehrman, *How Jesus*, 233.

9. Dixon, "Descending Spirit," 768, fn 35.

10. Edwards, "The Baptism," 44.

11 Dibelius, *From Tradition*, 273, fn 2; Bultmann, *History*, 251. See, for example, Gen. 1:2 (KJV): "And the Spirit of God moved upon the face of the waters." Its equivalent in the Jewish Study Bible (Tanakh translation) is: ". . . and a wind from God sweeping over the water—"

12. Edwards, "The Baptism," 47.

God's chosen in whom God takes delight, God says, "I have put my spirit upon him."

As for the symbolism of the dove, while there is no prior use of this symbol in Jewish literature, it had been used in Greek literature to denote the comings and goings of gods.[13] There are other instances in ancient mythology where a bird, most often a dove, was used to portray the infusion of divine power into an individual.[14] No matter what one may infer from these rich diverse interpretations of the baptism, there is little doubt that Mark uses the baptism story to introduce the beginning of God's eschatological kingdom, but he does so with well-known, culturally accepted mythical symbolism his audience would recognize.[15]

A New Teaching, With Authority

The one thing that all the diverse meanings found in the baptism story, whether they acknowledge Jesus as king, prophet, directly appointed by God, imbued with God's Spirit, or Son of God, have in common is that they confer on Jesus a divine spiritual authority. Mark emphasizes the bestowing of this authority early in his narrative by inserting two references to Jesus having "authority." At 1:22 he writes, "he taught them as one having authority, and not as the scribes," and at 1:27: "They were all amazed, and they kept on asking one another, 'What is this? A new teaching—with authority!'" (Note: that is a declarative sentence, not a question.) It is a rather odd response from the crowd, most likely one created by Mark. Immediately following this episode Jesus casts out demons. Early in his narrative Mark shows his audience that Jesus has authority over demons (1:27), authority to appoint others to have authority over demons (3:15), authority to forgive sins (2:10), and authority to change a part of the Law by redefining the Sabbath restrictions (2:28). In all these instances Jesus attributes the authority to do these things to the Son of Man, seemingly used here self-referentially, rather than claiming that he personally has the authority to act. Within chapters 1 and 2 Mark establishes Jesus' divine identity and the divine authority that derives from that identity.

---

13. Dixon, "Descending Spirits," 760, 780. Both Edwards, *The Baptism*, 47, and Dibelius, *From Tradition*, 273, support Dixon's claim regarding the absence of a dove as metaphor for God's Spirit in Jewish literature.

14. Bultmann, *History*, 249–50.

15. Edwards, "The Baptism," 43.

Boanerges

In chapter 3 we find the story of Jesus' appointment of the twelve apostles, including James and John, the sons of Zebedee, to whom Mark's Jesus curiously applies the appellation "*Boanerges, that is, Sons of Thunder*" (3:17). It is doubtful that this is anything but a Markan creation, but he neither follows up with an explanation as to why this strange epithet was applied to the brothers nor does he ever use the term again. On the surface it seems to be a useless bit of information. The traditional explanation, derived from Origen writing over 100 years later, holds that the brothers were so named because of their forceful—like thunder—preaching.[16] This *ex post facto* conclusion is logically weak and has little merit. A much more vigorous and verifiable explanation resides in pagan mythology.

"Sons of Thunder" would have reminded Mark's audience, Greek, Roman, and Jewish, of the *Dioscuri* who we know by their Latin names Castor and Pollux (Grk: *Polydeuces*), Greek brothers and gods whose names were given to the two brightest stars in the constellation Gemini. *Dioscuri*, derived from *Dion*, another Greek name for Zeus, means "Zeus' boys" or "Sons of Zeus." Zeus' other appellations[17] included the "Thunderer" or "Thundering One," and his father Cronus was known as "Father of Thunder and Lightning."[18] Homer introduces the twin brothers in Book 11 of the *Odyssey*:

> And I saw Leda next, Tyndareus' wife, who'd borne the king two sons, intrepid twins, Castor, breaker of horses, and the hardy boxer Polydeuces, both buried now in the life-giving earth though still alive. Even under the earth Zeus grants them that distinction: one day alive, the next day dead, each twin by turns, they both hold honors equal to the gods.[19]

Rendel Harris's 1913 book *Boanerges* is a comprehensive examination of the nearly universal pagan recognition of the birth of twins as a supernatural event. This belief arose out of the assumption that a spirit or god was involved in the fathering of one or both twins; if of one twin then the other was fathered by a mortal. As the legend of the Heavenly Twins developed, Zeus was thought to be the father of Pollux.[20] The Dioscuric cult has its

16. Harris, *Boanerges*, 2.

17. Zeus was also known as the "Sky God" and his offspring naturally shared that title. As such they controlled all "sky" events.

18. MacDonald, *The Homeric Epics*, 25.

19 Homer, *The Odyssey*.

20. MacDonald, *The Homeric Epics*, 29.

origin in primitive humankind's fear of both thunder and the birth of twins. The celestial booming of thunder and flashing of lethal lightening could only come from an all-powerful deity. Often, the birth of twins was seen as taboo, a bad omen requiring one or both infants to be discarded.[21] This original taboo morphed into a cult of worship of the Heavenly Twins[22] who could provide protection and good fortune in a variety of endeavors—war, horsemanship, hunting, fishing, farming, and sailing. Such twin-cults could be found in diverse cultures in Asia Minor, Europe, India, Scandinavia, Russia, Africa, and North and South America. The twin names differed, as did that of the paternal god, but the cult took on essentially the same characteristics. In the Greco-Roman world this cult of the "Heavenly Twins" became known as *Dioscurism*. Dioscurism not only became deeply rooted in both Hellenist and Jewish culture but also was well established throughout Europe before Christianity.[23] The burgeoning Christian church could not escape its influence.

References to the Dioscuri can be traced back to the most ancient of times in the Jewish culture. Harris identified a town in Western Palestine, near Jaffa, named Ibn Abraq or Ibraq, which means *Sons of Lightning*. Joshua 19:45 lists locations for the Tribe of Dan, including *Jehud* and *Bnē-Barqa*[24] and *Gath-rimmon*. "Here," Harris tells us, "we have the desired plural formation, *Sons of Lightning*, and curiously the [Assyrian] thunder-god, as Rimmon, is himself in the neighborhood."[25] The Dioscuri cult was also connected to the Maccabees.[26]

> The second book of Maccabees is a book which was written as late, perhaps, as the first years of the Christian era: it is decidedly Dioscurized: if the objection be made that it simply incorporates the work of Jason of Cyrene, the answer is that in that case we do not push Jewish Dioscurism back to an earlier date than about 100 B.C., and the events described are not themselves much earlier. So we bring Dioscurism practically down to our

21. The twins Romulus and Remus, fathered by the god Mars, were cast out to die but, nurtured by a she-wolf, survived to found Rome and achieve eternal veneration. Other notable twins include Amphion and Zethus, known for building Thebes, and Heracles and his brother Iphicles.

22. Harris, *Boanerges*, xviii–xx. Over time, the term "twins" included not only biological twins but also brothers who looked and acted alike and always sought equal treatment and reward; thus James and John could be considered Dioscouri.

23. Harris, *Boanerges*, xxi.

24. B'nē means "Sons of—" (Harris, *Boanerges*, 2.)

25. Harris, *Boanerges*, 198.

26. Harris, *Boanerges*, 289–90.

Lord's time, and this means that Dioscuric explanations cannot be wholly ruled out of the interpretation of events recoded in the Gospels . . .[27]

In folklore both brothers were exceptional horsemen, often referred to as "riders on swift horses," and venerated by soldiers in battle.[28] Mark's Jewish audience, therefore, would have been reminded of a scene in 2 Maccabees where, during a ferocious battle, the enemies of the Maccabees saw five men on horses with golden bridles appear out of heaven leading the Judeans. Two of the horsemen placed Judas Maccabees between them for protection and then, "They showered arrows and thunderbolts on the enemy so that confounded by blindness they fled in complete disorder" (2 Macc 10:30 NETS). Palestinian Dioscurism as a "cult prevailed in some form or tradition down to the Christian era"[29] and was active at a time coincident with the creation of the gospels.[30]

One of the main functions of the Dioscuri was the "protection of sailors in the Mediterranean and elsewhere."[31] Mariners venerated the Twin Gods, often sacrificing to them for safe journeys and protection while at sea. They believed them to be manifest in St. Elmo's fire, the phosphorescent glow that occasionally crept along the rigging of ships.[32] Expanding on Harris's research[33] we find this in *Homeric Hymn 33*:

> (T)he Sons of Zeus, glorious children of neat-ankled Leda, Castor the tamer of horses, and blameless Polydeuces. . . . children who are delivers of men on earth and of swift-going ships when stormy gales rage over the ruthless sea. Then the shipmen call upon the sons of great Zeus with vows of white lambs, going to the forepart of the prow; but the strong wind and the waves of the sea lay the ship under water, until suddenly these two are seen darting through the air on tawny wings. Forthwith they allay the blasts of the cruel winds and still the waves upon the surface of the white sea: fair signs are they and deliverance from toil. Hail, Tyndaridae, riders upon swift horses![34]

27. Harris, *Boanerges*, 288.

28. MacDonald, *The Homeric Epics*, 31.

29. Harris, *Boanerges*, 199.

30. Harris, *Boanerges*, 290.

31. Harris, *Boanerges*, xxi.

32. MacDonald, *The Homeric Epics*, 26.

33. Harris, *Boanerges*, 285.

34. *Homeric Hymn* 33, "To the Dioscuri," 15–19. The author of the Homeric Hymns is unknown. They are a collection of Greek hymns celebrating their gods and are

Mark's chapter 4 contains the story of "a great windstorm" on, presumably, the Sea of Galilee. This body of water likely got its name from the Aramaic word for waves, *galelē*, because it is uniquely prone to sudden swells created by strong winds being funneled through the surrounding hills.[35] Considering the pervasiveness of Dioscurism throughout Palestine and the veneration of the Heavenly Twins as protectors for men who go to sea, such as fishermen, Mark's audience would have been quick to arrive at the following logical syllogism: only those of divine nature, like the Dioscuri, can quell a storm at sea; Jesus quells a storm at sea; therefore, Jesus must have a divine nature. Whether this pericope is a historical fact or a Markan creation, perhaps based on Psalm 107:23–30, it serves to further Mark's goal of proving Jesus was divine.

The Acts of the Apostles 28:11 informs us that while on his way to Rome Paul was shipwrecked on Malta. When he was able to continue his journey he did so on "an Alexandrian ship with the Twin Brothers as its figurehead" (NRSV). The KJV version specifically states that the Alexandrian ship's "sign was Castor and Pollux." Why would the Gospel writers mention such a seemingly insignificant detail as the figurehead? While modern readers would pay little attention to the description, a first-century audience would have found that reference to the Twin Brothers profoundly important, an indication that after that first near-fatal voyage Paul was now under the protection of the Dioscuri.

That Jesus held James and John, the Boanerges, in high regard is evident by their being among the select few to be asked to witness both his raising of Jarius's daughter and the Transfiguration. The Dioscuri were likewise held in high regard in both Greek and Roman cultures as evidenced by their being depicted on numerous coins, paintings, and reliefs sitting one on the left and one on the right basking in the glory of one of the Olympian gods.[36] In Mark 10:37 James and John ask Jesus if they could have the honor of sitting one on his right hand and one on his left when he comes into his glory. Mark's audience would have instantly recognized the Dioscuric connection—if James and John are Boanerges and are to sit at the right and left of Jesus, then this Jesus must be a god.

"Homeric" only in the sense that they reflect Homer's style of writing.

35. Harris, *Boanerges*, 281.

36. MacDonald, *The Homeric Epics*, 27.

Caesarea Philippi

Analyzing Mark's Gospel according to Aristotle's plot criteria (complication, unraveling (denouement), reversal of intention, recognition, and tragic incident) of a tragedy, we find that the complex themes found in the first seven chapters—establishing Jesus' identity and authority, maintaining the messianic secret, the baptism, miracles, exorcisms, and teachings—form the complication, defined as "all that extends from the beginning of the action to the part which marks the turning-point to good or bad fortune."[37] Mark's chapter 8 marks the beginning of the *unraveling (denouement)*, which is simply all that remains of the story to the end. Peter's acknowledgment of Jesus as the Messiah (8:27–33) vividly demonstrates Aristotle's concept of *recognition*:

> Recognition . . . is a change from ignorance to knowledge, producing love or hate between the persons destined by the poet for good or bad fortune . . . and the recognition which is most intimately connected with the plot and action is, as we have said, the recognition of persons.[38] But of all recognitions, the best is that which arises from the incidents themselves, where the startling discovery is made by natural means.[39]

The importance of this scene is marked by the fact that it is located in the middle of Mark's Gospel. It was typical in Greek drama about immortals to reserve that position for the change-event where the plot would suddenly take a new course—Aristotle's reversal of intention.[40] In this scene Mark incorporates the two most powerful elements of emotional interest in a tragic drama—reversal of intention and recognition.[41] What occurs in the confrontation between Peter and Jesus is a move away from Markan insinuation of Jesus as Messiah to a stated recognition by Peter that Jesus is the Messiah. We have acknowledged that identification is a dominant theme in Mark and identification necessitates recognition, and recognition is one of the most powerful elements driving the plot. Greek dramatists often masked the identity of the protagonist in their mythic stories until such time as recognition was needed for the protagonist to meet his or her fate. From that change-event forward the pre-existing tension between two conflicting elements begins to hasten toward some inevitable resolution—Aristotle's tragic incident.

37. Aristotle, *Poetics*, 18.1.

38. Aristotle, *Poetics*, 11.2.

39. Aristotle, *Poetics*, 16.6.

40. Dawsey, *Peter's Last Sermon*, 35–36.

41. Aristotle, *Poetics*, 6.5, 11.3.

Readers are grabbed by the new revelation and pulled along with growing speculation about how the story will end.

This requisite theme of recognition in Greek literature is evident in Mark's narrative, and he delivers it bluntly with the Jesus-Peter confrontation at Caesarea Philippi. Since Jesus as all-knowing God would have been aware of who people thought him to be, his question, "Who do people say that I am?" (v27), seems unnecessary. Mark, however, uses the question to trigger all that follows. Here we have Aristotle's reversal of intention, "a change by which the action veers round to its opposite."[42] The messianic secret begins to unravel. After 9:9 Jesus gives no more prohibitions about his identity; indeed, at 9:14–29 he exorcizes a demon in front of a large crowd, including some scribes, without a command to secrecy. From that point Mark is working toward the Passion Narrative. Soon Jesus would enter Jerusalem to the "Hosannas" of a welcoming crowd. No more secrecy because now his public recognition is essential to the passion plan. He can only hope that his disciples have come to understand who he is and what is about to happen.

Jesus jolts Peter into an open admission that he is the Messiah. When Peter acknowledges that Jesus is the Messiah we do not know what concept of the Messiah Peter held. Obviously, the suffering-rejected-eventually executed Messiah Jesus claimed to be did not fit Peter's messianic schema. From his response it is obvious that Peter totally rejected the concept of a suffering Messiah, leaving the likelihood that he still clung to the Judaic schema of Messiah as conquering hero, or as *theios aner*. It is also quite obvious that neither he nor the other apostles comprehended the suffering-servant role of Jesus nor of true discipleship. Jesus and Peter held differing views of messiahship.[43] Little by little, Mark has deftly built up his audience's recognition of Jesus as the Messiah, but one who is different from traditional Judaic expectations.

With the event at Caesarea Philippi Mark makes it clear that those *in* the narrative are aware that Jesus is more than a prophet, that he is the Messiah—of some sort. Chapter 8 marks a dramatic change. In succeeding events (9:33–37; 10:32–40) Mark puts more emphasis on the suffering-servant motif as the disciples struggle to grasp both the full nature of Jesus' messiahship and of discipleship. After Caesarea Philippi, Mark's Gospel enters the denouement phase and events start moving rapidly toward the tragic incident—the passion.

---

42. Aristotle, *Poetics*, 11.1.

43. Weeden, "The Heresy," 146–47.

Transfiguration

Some scholars assert that the transfiguration story (Mark 9:2–10) was originally a post-resurrection event previously existing in the pre-Markan tradition that Mark moved to precede the Passion Narrative.[44] Robert Stein disputes that claim.[45] We must accept, however, that, since Mark did not write events in chronological order, this event may have happened at any time during or after Jesus' earthly ministry. At Caesarea Philippi Peter *says* Jesus is the Messiah; at the Transfiguration Mark *shows* Jesus is the Messiah. The two events are close enough in Mark's narrative to suspect that he had purpose for placing the transfiguration story where he did.

For Mark's Jewish audience, the inclusion of Moses in the transfiguration story would have brought to mind Exodus 24, where Moses ascends Mt. Sinai to receive the Ten Commandments. The two narratives have much in common: Moses, selection of three associates, the cloud covering, the "glory" of the Lord, the "six days," audible communication with God, building of altars, and offering of sacrifices. Mark's Hellenistic audience, however, might have drawn similarities from a different source. MacDonald[46] thinks it is to be found in "Homeric Hymn 5, To Aphrodite," where Anchises encounters the goddess Aphrodite who comes to him from the clouds:

> And Aphrodite, the daughter of Zeus, stood before him, being like a pure maiden in height and mien, that he should not be frightened when he took heed of her with his eyes. Now when Anchises saw her, he marked her well and wondered at her mien and bright and shining garments. For she was clad in a robe out-shining the brightness of fire, a splendid robe of gold, enriched with all manner of needlework, which shimmered like the moon over her tender breasts, a marvel to see. And Anchises was seized with love, and said to her, ". . . maybe you are one of the Graces come hither, who bear the gods company and are called immortal," (75-105).

Although Anchises recognizes her as an immortal, she denies it (another incidence of divine anonymity). Despite her denial Anchises says, "I will make you an altar upon a high peak in a far seen place and will sacrifice rich offerings to you at all seasons."[47] In this Homeric Hymn, which would have been available to Mark, we find details that parallel the transfiguration

44. Weeden, *Mark: Traditions,* 119–24; Bultmann, *History,* 259.

45. Stein, "Is the Transfiguration," 83, 91.

46. MacDonald, *The Homeric Epics,* 93.

47 *Homeric Hymn* 5, 91–105.

scene: a divine person coming from the clouds shrouded in divine radiance, communication between a deity and mortals, the offer to build altars and make sacrifices. Jesus tells his apostles not to reveal his divinity, and Aphrodite denies her divinity.

The Markan Apocalypse

Chapter 13 is profoundly important in Mark's Gospel. It not only gives us discernible examples of Mark's redaction activity but also insight into the *Sitz im Leben* of both Mark and the primitive church at the time of his writing. This portion of the Gospel takes the form of a *vaticinum ex eventu*,[48] which is the presentation of actual past events known by the author who then presents them as a prophecy given before those events occurred. One might say that it is a prophecy in hindsight. It is well-accepted that Mark's chapter 13 is a composition of his own making,[49] with much of the material taken from existing Jewish apocalyptic material.[50] Although many of the elements within the chapter have historic legitimacy, as an extract of an actual event in Jesus' ministry it is fictitious. Because it foretells of "end time" events, this particular chapter is also referred to as *The Markan Apocalypse*,[51] *Little Apocalypse*,[52] and *The Synoptic Apocalypse*.[53] Mark has combined pre-existing Jewish Apocalyptic prophecies with specific Christian ideas in an attempt to justify the primitive church's emerging Christology.[54] It is a very controversial section of Mark's Gospel and the subject of multiple, sometimes opposing, theories.[55] One thing that many scholars do agree on, however, is that this chapter offers evidence that allows us to determine more precisely when Mark wrote this Gospel.

Both Weeden and Marxsen analyze Mark 13 insightfully and in detail. What is offered here is a general survey of their findings. Marxsen breaks the chapter down into Jewish Apocalyptic verses (7, 8, 12, 14–22, 24–27),

---

48. Weeden, *Mark: Traditions,*72; Bultmann, *History*, 122.

49. Marxsen, *Mark the Evangelist*, 161.

50. Bultmann, *History*, 125.

51. Marxsen, *Mark the Evangelist*, 151

52. Brandon, *The Trial of Jesus,*71.

53. Bultmann, *History*, 122.

54. Bultmann, *History*, 125.

55. Hatina, "The Focus of Mark," 47, disagrees with the apocalyptic interpretation of this chapter. Instead, he sees it as a prophesy of the destruction of the temple given as a *paranesis*, that is, a farewell address.

and Christian verses (5–6, 9–11, 13a, 23, 28–37).[56] Weeden's analysis notes evidence of Mark's *Sitz im Leben* generally corresponding to those verses identified by Marxsen as being Christian, more or less corroborating the conclusion that events within the Christian church influenced Mark's redaction of this chapter.[57] Let us turn our interest to some of the specific prophecies to which Mark draws his audience's attention.

This chapter opens with the disciples commenting on the largeness of the stones and of the Temple buildings. Jesus' reply, a reply that will be used to incriminate him later, is to say that as large as those buildings and stones are, they will be "thrown down" (v. 2). The disciples are curious as to when that may happen, thus giving Mark's Jesus the opportunity to again teach his disciples in private (vv. 3–5). Jesus then commences with his apocalyptic predictions. Following the prediction of the Temple's destruction (v. 2), he predicts the appearance of false prophets (vv. 5–6, 21–22); wars and rumors of wars, natural disasters, tribulations (vv.7–9); family disintegration (v.12); persecution of his followers (vv.9, 13); desolation and sacrilege (v.14); a warning to flee (vv.14b–20). By the time Mark wrote his Gospel, nearly all those things had actually occurred prior to or during the Jewish uprising of 66–70 CE. In Books 5–7 of his *The Jewish War* (written sometime in the 70s CE), Josephus gives an extensive confirmation of these actual events, some of which he witnessed firsthand, that befell Jerusalem during the war including famine, rise of false prophets, family members turning on one another (including cannibalism), utter chaos within Jerusalem, the Diaspora of the Jews and Christians out of Jerusalem, and the destruction of the Temple. Earthquakes in Phrygia in 61 CE and Pompeii in 62 CE would account for the reference to extraordinary natural occurrences (Mark 24–25).[58] And we know of the persecutions referenced in vv. 9, 11, and 13 endured by the Christians during the Neronian persecutions. The prophecy of "nation rising against nation and kingdom against kingdom" (v. 8) was obviously a reference to the war between Rome and Judea.[59] These were actual events that Mark and his audience would have known and Mark utilized to project his theology, especially the coming of the Son of Man at the end of time (vv. 26–27)—the Parousia.

Verse 14, known as the *abomination of desolation* passage, is a complex challenge to modern readers and has given rise to competing theories as to

56. Marxsen, *Mark the Evangelist*, 161–62.

57. Weeden, *Mark: Traditions*, 73.

58. Marxsen, *Mark the Evangelist*, 173–74.

59. This may also have been a veiled reference to the clash between the incoming kingdom of God and the kingdom of non-believers.

what Mark was referring with the "abomination of desolation." The passage opens with Jesus saying: "But when you see the desolating sacrilege set up where it ought not to be (let the reader understand), then those in Judea must flee to the mountains." This statement is suggestive of similar sayings in Daniel where reference is made to such abominable desolations (Dan 9:26–27; 11:31; 12:11). In addition to the connection with Daniel, we find Jesus' statement also has a connection with 1 Maccabees 1:54: "And on the fifteenth day of the month Chaseleu, in the hundred and forty-fifth year, he [Antiochus] constructed an abomination of desolation on the altar."

Those comments found in both Daniel and 1 Maccabees are in reference to the sacrilegious activities of Antiochus Epiphanies and add another link between Daniel, Maccabees, and Mark. As for the parenthetical comment "(let the reader understand)," the only instance in the Gospel where Mark addresses his audience directly, we have a parallel in Daniel 8:17: "Understand, O mortal,[60] that the vision is for the time of the end." Fleeing to the mountains is not an uncommon Jewish response to threats. In 2 Maccabees 5:27 Judas Maccabees and nine companions flee to the mountains; in 1 Maccabees 2:28 Matthias and his sons do likewise. Mark's Jewish audience would have been quick to relate Jesus' statement to both Daniel and Maccabees. The impact of Jesus' statement, however, would not have ended there because, "But when you see the desolating sacrilege set up where it ought not to be . . ." would have reminded Mark's audience of more recent outrageous events. In 71 CE, the year following the fall of Jerusalem, the conquering Roman generals Vespasian and his son Titus returned to Rome to lead the traditional grand triumphal parade. Of this spectacle Josephus, who witnessed it first hand, writes:

> Vespasian resolved to build a temple to Peace . . . he also laid up therein those golden vessels and instruments that were taken out of the Jewish temple, as ensigns of his glory. But still he gave order that they should lay up their Law, and the purple veils of the holy place, in the royal palace itself, and keep them there. (J.W. 7.5, 7)

One theory holds that with something being set up where "it ought not to be" Mark was referring to the Temple artifacts taken from the holy sanctuary of God now irreverently displayed in a temple of the pagan Roman emperor. A competing theory holds that it relates to an event in 70 CE when, as the Temple was being destroyed, the Roman legionnaires set up their standards and hailed Titus as divine emperor; in other words, it was

60. In some translations "mortal" is rendered as "Son of Man," which means "human" in this instance.

Titus being worshipped within the confines of the Temple that was sacrilegious.[61] This latter incident may be what Eusebius had in mind when he wrote of the last days of the war, "Finally, the abomination of desolation, according to the prophetic declaration, stood in the very temple of God" (*EH* 3.5). Regardless, Mark certainly would have known of these events occurring, as they did, before he wrote his Gospel; therefore, we can conclude with a high degree of confidence that Mark wrote his Gospel no earlier than 70 CE, most likely in 71 CE.[62]

The remaining portion of this chapter (vv. 26–36) is a blend of Jewish apocalyptic tradition and Christian christological beliefs related to end time events. It is easy to recognize the corresponding references to the coming of the Son of Man[63] in Mark 13:26 and Daniel 7:13 (KJV). Additionally, similarities abound in the list of things portending the end of times (Mark 13:14–27) compared to Gabriel's revelation of end time events as he cautions Daniel: "Listen, and I will tell you what will take place later in the period of wrath, for it refers to the appointed time of the end" (Dan 8:19). There is a strong correlation between the last portion of Mark's chapter 13 and the prophetic announcements in Daniel 9:11–13 concerning the end of Jerusalem. Mark's Jewish audience would have been well-versed in Daniel's apocalyptic warnings. They could not have received the news of the suffering of Jerusalem during the war as reported in Josephus's eyewitness report: "That neither did any other city ever suffer such miseries, nor did any age ever breed a generation more fruitful in wickedness than this was, from the beginning of the world" (*J.W.* 5.10, 5), without recalling Daniel 9:12: "He has confirmed his words, which he spoke against us and against our rulers, by bringing upon us a calamity so great that what has been done against Jerusalem has never before been done under the whole heaven."

Surely it all added up to the beginning of the end!

By 71 CE Mark saw both his Jewish world and his Christian world disintegrating. His Jewish world had suffered a demoralizing defeat in war, its inhabitants suffered merciless tribulations and were forced to flee their homes. Jerusalem and the Temple lay in ruins. His church world was likewise shattered and in flight, challenged by false messiahs and persecutions. The obvious explanation for all these disasters could be found in the prophecies in Daniel—these signs pointed to the fact that the end time was coming soon. And had not Jesus promised that it would occur during their

---

61. Brandon, *The Trial of Jesus*, 72.

62. Brandon, *The Trial of Jesus*, 68; Conzelmann, "History and Theology," 187; Dibelius, *From Tradition*, 10.

63. "Human being" in NRSV and in the Jewish Study Bible Tanakh translation.

generation (9:1, 13:30)? Mark needed to convince his audience that their hope and salvation lay in finding meaning in the crucifixion of the poor miracle-working Galilean who suffered and was executed as a common rebel. Given traditional Jewish beliefs that was a nearly impossible task. To continue building his case that Jesus was the divine Messiah, Mark very adroitly blended traditional Jewish apocalyptic beliefs, actual world events, and the needs of the new church into his own theology.

Chapters 14–16 include the Passion Narrative and the ending of Mark's Gospel. Those are subjects of great complexity and importance and will be examined separately in the next two chapters.

8

The Passion Narrative

The Tragic Incident is a destructive or painful action, such as death . . . bodily agony, wounds and the like.

—ARISTOTLE, *POETICS*

THE FIRST FORMAL REFERENCE we have of a passion event, that is, Jesus' death, burial, resurrection, and post-resurrection events, comes to us from Paul.[1]

> For I handed on to you as of first importance what I in turn had received: that Christ died for our sins in accordance with the scriptures, and that he was buried, and that he was raised on the third day in accordance with the scriptures, and that he appeared to Cephas, then to the Twelve (1 Cor 15: 3–5).

Although Paul does not tell us when, how, or from whom he received it, the fact that he did receive it prior to 55 CE (the approximate date of 1 Corinthians[2]), indicates that the Passion Narrative existed in some form many years prior to Mark's writing.

1. Hamilton, "Resurrection Tradition," 415.
2. Lea and Black, *The New Testament*, 408.

While some scholars would start Mark's Passion Narrative at chapter 11, it is more generally accepted that it is in chapters 14 and 15 that we find the first detailed written account of the passion event.[3] In all four Gospels the essentials of the Passion Narrative (anointing, supper, Gethsemane, trial, betrayal, crucifixion, death, and burial) are quite similar, leading to a widely held belief that it was already circulating in a consolidated form during the oral tradition. The Passion Narrative is the only chronological (suffered, died, buried) order-of-events story that emerges from the oral tradition.[4] It is a continuing plot building up to a climax in the crucifixion (Aristotle's Tragic Incident) and an epilogue in the Easter event.

What we read in the Synoptics, however, is not an unedited tradition story about the passion. Indeed, many scholars have concluded that much in Mark's Passion Narrative is his creation or, at least, heavily redacted.[5] This conclusion is derived from both historical and textual inconsistencies. The fact that Jesus was summarily executed indicates that there must have been some sort of official hearing that led to a death sentence. The challenge is to separate historical fact from theological purpose. Regardless of the commonalities found in the four renderings of the Passion Narrative, there are still differences enough to indicate that each of the Evangelists added insertions and creative content to fit his theological viewpoint.[6] What Paul wrote in 1 Corinthians 15: 3–5 more than twenty years after the crucifixion, and fifteen years before Mark, contained the foundation of the original Passion Narrative—Christ died, was buried, and was raised. From there, the passion story evolved during the interim years. John Dominic Crossan opines that it is possible that the very first Christians did not even know the details of the passion.[7] In Mark's Passion Narrative we find clues for what came out of tradition, how much he created, and why he created what he did. What need of the early church did he see that had to be resolved? While there is much to be examined in the Passion Narrative, we will focus on the anointing, the Eucharistic meal, the events in Gethsemane, the trial, and the crucifixion.

3. Nickelsburg, "The Genre," 164.

4. Dibelius, *From Tradition*, 180; Stein, *Studying*, 178; Piper, "The Origin," 123.

5. Brandon, *The Trial of Jesus*, 106; Bultmann, *History*, 269–71; Crossan, *Jesus: A Revolutionary*, 140–43; Dibelius, *From Tradition*, 178–217; Donahue, *Are You the Christ?* 53–54.

6. Donahue, *Are You the Christ?* 7–8.

7. Crossan, *Jesus: A Revolutionary*, 145.

The Anointing and the Last Supper

Mark uses the anointing (14:3–9) to foreshadow the approaching burial of Jesus, symbolically anointing the dead, as well as alluding to the traditional anointing reserved for the kings of Israel.[8] The account of the Last Supper (14:22–25) presents a challenge. The Evangelists differ in their presentation of this event. Mark presents it merely as a last meal, not as a Passover meal.[9] Paul simply refers to the meal as occurring, "on the night he was betrayed" (1 Cor 11:23). Bultmann concludes that the eventual recognition of this last supper as a Passover meal was due to a later editorial revision.[10] The New Testament account of this meal as Eucharistic, arguably the crown jewel of Christian rituals, is due more to theological necessity than historical fact. A fellowship meal of bread-breaking and -sharing was common practice for Mark's audience.[11] Additionally, many religious cults at that time shared the belief that participants could consume their god at ritual meals;[12] therefore, as the Christology of the primitive church progressed, transforming this last meal into an indispensible theological ritual would have encountered little disagreement.

Mark makes no mention that the ritual should be repeated in remembrance, nor does he mention either atonement for sin or any saving significance of the event. Mark avoids relating blood-letting to redemption for sin, writing only, "This is my blood of the covenant, which is poured out for many" (14:24). Adela Yarbro Collins clarifies the "blood of the covenant" as being a reference to the ceremonial covenant ratification found in Exodus 24:3–8, which had nothing to do with sin, but rather establishes a covenant (in Mark, Jesus) with God.[13] Paul also mentions this new covenant in 1 Corinthians 11:25 and directs the ritual to be repeated in remembrance of Jesus but without attaching atonement for sin. Years later Matthew expanded this to: "Drink from it, all of you, for this is my blood of the covenant, which is poured out for many for the forgiveness of sins" (Matt 26:28). Because bread-breaking was common practice in first-century culture, Jesus' words regarding the bread reflect an historic reality. Due to the Orthodox Jewish revulsion of blood, however, the reference to the cup of wine as blood would

8. Only women anointed the dead (Ehrman, *How Jesus*, 167); thus the historical logic of the women being first to arrive at Jesus' tomb.

9. Dibelius, *From Tradition*, 182; Beck, "The Last Supper," 194, fn. 6.

10. Bultmann, *History*, 265–266.

11. Beck, "The Last Supper," 193.

12. González, *A History*, 56.

13. Collins, "Finding Meaning," 176.

have been much less likely.[14] This aversion of blood is noted in Genesis 9:4, Leviticus 17:14 and 15:19–33. Deuteronomy 12:23–27 gives specific prohibitions against the consumption of blood. We find this prohibition again in Acts 15:29, where it is decided that Gentiles can be counted among the believers and saved without being circumcised as long as they "abstain from what has been sacrificed to idols *and from blood*" (italics added). Moreover, chapters 9 and 10 of the *Didache*, the primitive church's guide for the performance of church rituals, including the Eucharistic meal, makes no mention of the bread as Jesus' body, the wine as Jesus' blood, or any insinuation of atonement. It simply describes this meal as one of thanksgiving to God for opening his kingdom through Jesus; again, Jesus as covenant. Indications are that, although certain features of the Last Supper are based on facts, over all the Evangelists co-opted the event to advance an evolving theology. We must, therefore, consider that, in due course, theological purpose influenced subsequent Christian interpretive schema of the details Mark portrayed in his Last Supper account.

Gethsemane

As regards the Gethsemane scene, there are two particular themes worth noting: betrayal and abandonment. Judas was not the only culprit involved in Jesus' betrayal. While historic animosity falls on Judas as betrayer, we should consider that abandonment and (Peter's) denial are also forms of betrayal—especially when the disciples pledged not to betray Jesus (Mark 14:19). Although theories abound regarding the meaning of the insertion of the "young man" wrapped only in a linen cloth (14:51–52) who loses that cloth as he escapes the clutches of the arresting mob, none of them have gained traction. Some assume him to be an angel, the same angel that appears at the empty tomb, although Mark does not assert either fact. This incident, found only in Mark, seems an absurd insertion since it needlessly interrupts the Gethsemane scene and adds nothing to the plot. Some have theorized that it was Mark himself[15]—a totally unsubstantiated conclusion. Why would he interject something completely unrelated (and somewhat capricious) into a dramatic scene of such profound consequence? And yet, Mark had some purpose for inserting this incident. My theory is that the young man is a symbol of *life*. Consider that the purpose of the "arresting" mob was not to arrest Jesus but to kill him (Mark 14:1, 3:6, 11:18). It was their fear of Jesus'

14. Beck, "The Last Supper," 195–96; Dibelius, *From Tradition,*207; Williams, *Jesus' Death*, 208.

15. Lea and Black, *The New Testament*, 141.

supporters that prevented them from doing it openly (Mark 14:2); therefore, they came at night when their murderous plan could be carried out unseen. But when Jesus' supporters put up a fight (Mark 14:47) the arresting mob encountered the very resistance they feared and backed down from murder. At that moment life, like the young man, escapes the clutches of death. If we jump ahead to Mark 16:5 where the women enter the tomb and find a "young man dressed in a white robe" who informs them Jesus has risen, he is alive. Life again has defeated death. Mark never identifies the young man at the tomb as an angel. That we have come to designate him as one is, first of all, a schema-filling attempt to give him an identity that Mark fails to give while underwriting the divine symbolism of the empty tomb. Secondly, it is simply a projection carried over from the other Gospels. The appearance of the young man at the tomb has a striking similarity to Daniel (12:6–7) when Daniel has a vision of a "man clothed in linen." Both Daniel and Mark bring their narratives to closure with similar visions.

The Trial

Because Mark's audience would have quickly recognized an excessive deviation from the pre-existing Passion Narrative, he had to preserve the kerygmatic framework of that traditional story while maintaining his pursuit of proving Jesus was the Messiah. And yet, the trial, sentencing, and execution could not be ignored. Mark's conundrum was twofold. First, up to this point in his narrative his portrayal of the Romans had been favorable (see chapter 6, *Political Considerations*), but now he had to justify that with the fact that Jesus was condemned to death for sedition by the Roman Procurator Pontius Pilate. To avoid implicating Roman involvement in the crucifixion, Mark obfuscates the entirely Roman-sanctioned execution for sedition behind the Sanhedrin's accusation of blasphemy. He does not achieve this goal logically or seamlessly. He does, however, use the trial to advance a more messianic theology and lay blame for Jesus' execution on the Jews.

Immediately after the arrest in Gethsemane Jesus is taken to the "high priest;[16] and all the chief priests, the elders and the scribes" (14:53). That the entire Sanhedrin formally met not only at night but also at the house of the high priest is historically unlikely.[17] It would be comparable to the U.S. Supreme Court holding a hearing at night at the home of the Chief Justice. The scene, however, allows Mark to implicate the Jewish authorities. The trial

---

16. Caiaphas was the high priest and remained so during Pilate's ten-year (26 to 36 CE) tenure as governor.

17. Brandon, *The Trial of Jesus*, 87.

(Mark 14:55–64) begins with the attempt to charge Jesus with threatening to destroy the Temple. We must question the origin of this accusation, for nowhere does Mark attribute to Jesus a direct threat to destroy the Temple, (13:2 is not a direct threat), not even when he chased out the money changers. Actually, his actions of chasing out the money changers indicates he wanted to preserve the Temple as the house of God, not to destroy it. Threatening to destroy the Temple was a threat to destroy something of God and, therefore, may have been viewed as blasphemous.[18] But this charge quickly collapses with witnesses giving either false or conflicting testimony (14:59). Mark strengthens his portrayal of Jesus as the innocent sufferer by creating certain allegations and then showing them to be false.

Under Roman rule blasphemy was the only indictment for which Jews could put someone to death and stoning the only method allowed.[19] So the Sanhedrin failed in this attempt to legitimize their right to put Jesus to death. The true Messiah could not be guilty of blasphemy nor of threatening to destroy the Temple, so Mark had to rationalize another way of getting to the crucifixion and still mitigate Roman complicity in the execution. Without substantiated proof that Jesus had threatened the Temple the high priest had to take another approach. At 14:61–62 we find a Markan insertion. The high priest asks Jesus: "Are you the Messiah, the Son of the Blessed One?" Mark uses the situation and the dialog to both affirm Jesus as Messiah: "I am." (14:62),[20] and give the high priest the pretense of blasphemy he had been seeking. Our modern understanding of "blasphemy" is quite different from that of Mark's audience. Collins explains that a more exact translation of the Aramaic and corresponding Greek term used here by Mark is "speaks insolently."[21] While Mark's audience can see that the charge of blasphemy was trumped up, they may have also recognized in Jesus' terse reply an insolent blasphemous-like response. Now the high priest had evidence, albeit quite weak, of blasphemy.

Again, if the charge of blasphemy was valid, the Jews had the right to stone Jesus to death. Instead they take him to Pilate (15:1). Why? Because Mark could not alter the well-known historical fact that the Romans executed Jesus for sedition. If the chief priests, elders, scribes, and the whole council did meet in a subsequent morning session (15:1), it is conceivable

18. Collins, "The Charge," 381. Knowledge of the first-century Jewish nuances of *blasphemy* greatly illuminates Mark's scene. See Collins' article.

19. Dibelius, *From Tradition*, 214; Brandon, *The Trial of Jesus*, 90. Based on Leviticus 24:16.

20. The "I am" response is significant because it is the identifier God uses for himself in Ex 3:14.

21. Collins, *The Charge*, 385.

that the chief priests used this time to concoct the many other accusations (15:3–4) they presented to Pilate in hopes of obtaining a death sentence. When they get to Pilate the charge of blasphemy (a Jewish problem) simply disappears and Mark replaces it with a charge ripe with political threat (a Roman problem): "Pilate asked him, 'Are you the king of the Jews?'" (15:2), to which Jesus replies, "You say so," (another rather insolent reply). In reality, this is all Pilate needed to hear to sentence him to death. But from 15:4 to 15:15 Mark depicts a Pilate reluctant to crucify a *seemingly* self-admitted insurrectionist. Such reluctance contradicts the Pilate described in Josephus's first-hand account as notoriously cruel, so cruel, in fact, that he was eventually called back to Rome (*Ant.* 18.4, 2). It does, however, allow Mark to provide cover for the Romans and portray the Jews as the culprits in the execution of their Messiah. Through Pilate's incredulity, "Why, what evil has he done?" (15:14), Mark minimizes Pilate's, that is, Rome's, involvement and further projects Jesus as the innocent suffering martyr. Jesus' encounter with Pilate has distinctive similarities to that of Shadrach, Meshach, and Abednego before Nebuchadnezzar in Daniel 3:14–18,[22] another reference to the Maccabean motif of the suffering servant.

Barabbas

Evidence points to the fact that Mark created the Barabbas (bar Abbas) story.[23] There is no reference in any extant Roman or Jewish records or historical accounts that the Romans ever released a prisoner for any Jewish festival.[24] And, as we have come to know, Pilate's characteristic brutality contradicts such an act. Little to no concern for Jewish sensibilities can be found in the history of the Roman occupation or, especially, in Pilate's reign where there was even the slightest hint of rebellion. Mark uses the Barabbas story to further Jewish culpability for Jesus' death while minimizing Roman involvement.

Although the Barabbas episode is a Markan insertion used to fill a literary purpose, he may have had a valid reason for creating and inserting it where he did. Mark makes brief mention that Barabbas was in prison with other rebels involved in a recent insurrection (15:7). The Romans were well aware of the fact that Passover was a celebration of Jewish freedom

22. Nickelsburg, "The Genre," 172.

23. Aslan, *Zealot*, 149; Brandon, *The Trial*, 113; Bultmann, *History*, 272; Crossan, *Jesus: A Revolutionary*, 141.

24. Aslan, *Zealot*, 149; Crossan, *Jesus: A Revolutionary*, 141; MacDonald, *The Homeric Epics*, 40.

from Egyptian bondage and each year's celebration would stir passions for independence from Roman control. It is conceivable that Jesus' Temple-cleansing antics were viewed as part of the insurrection Mark mentions, thus justifying his arrest and allowing Mark to put Jesus' arrest into an existing historical context known to his audience.

Crucifixion and Burial

Crucifixion, sometimes referred to as *bodily suspension* in ancient texts, was a well-established and common form of execution for many ancient Middle Eastern cultures before and during the first century CE.[25] It was a form of execution that the Romans used extensively. For the reasons given below, it was nearly always used for those perceived to be a threat to Roman rule—and the Romans were not in the least reluctant to use it. General Varus crucified 2,000 rebels involved in a previous uprising (*Ant.* 17.10.1); in the 66 CE uprising troops under the command of Florus, the procurator of Judea, executed 3,600 men, women, and children, many by crucifixion (Josephus *J.W.* 2.14.9); during the final siege of Jerusalem in 70 CE Titus' troops captured and crucified as many as 500 Jewish resisters a day, and "nailed those they caught, one after one way, and another after another, to the crosses, by way of jest, when their multitude was so great, that room was wanting for the crosses, and crosses wanting for the bodies" (*J.W.* 5.11.1). And as forerunner to such cruelty must be added Nero's crucifixion of thousands of Christians wrongly accused of starting the great fire in Rome.

Crucifixion was designed to do three things. It would seem obvious that its primary purpose was the ensuing slow, agonizing death caused by the lethal posture imposed by hanging on the cross. Often, however, the victim was already dead, executed and then hanged on the cross, which implicates two other Roman intentions for using it—humiliation and intimidation. The victim, alive or dead, was stripped naked and crucified in a public area, such as a crossroads, busy road, a hill, anywhere widely open to public view. Thirdly, the public nature of the spectacle was meant to intimidate anyone who might consider challenging Roman rule. To drive home both the humiliating and deterrent purposes for crucifixion burial was rarely permitted. In those extremely rare instances when burial was permitted it was either in recognition of an important Roman holiday, like the emperor's birthday, or for someone whose family had political clout.[26]

---

25. Chapman, "Perceptions of Crucifixion," 313–16.

26. Ehrman, *How Jesus*, 159. Evans, "Jewish Burial Traditions," 233, contends the Romans sometimes allowed burial except during times of rebellion. Mark 15:7 tells us

Proper burial was sacred to nearly all ancient Middle Eastern cultures, especially the Jews. To deny it was to deny religious/spiritual closure. In Jesus' case this was especially crucial because the Jews would have strictly adhered to Deuteronomy 21:23 regarding the corpse of one hanged for a crime: "His corpse must not remain all night upon the tree; you must bury him that same day, for anyone hung on a tree is under God's curse." Mark had to get Jesus off the cross. In its use of crucifixion the Romans paid little heed to Jewish customs or concerns. Why would they crucify someone for sedition in the morning and then have a compassionate change of heart that same afternoon? The corpse was meant to remain in public view, serving as carrion for birds and beasts, and a warning to others. Eventually, the bones ended up either in a common pit or, most often, left on the open ground;[27] hence the name *Golgotha* ("place of a skull," Mark 15:22), may derive from its shape but just as likely from the skulls left exposed there. The Romans used crucifixion to physically, psychologically, and religiously brutalize its foes. Mark's crucifixion story offers embellishments above and beyond the realities of Roman crucifixion practices.

There are, however, aspects of Mark's crucifixion story that may be accepted as historically accurate because they fit the general pattern for what is known about Roman crucifixions. These would include the scourging, which was part of the crucifixion process; Jesus may have needed help carrying the cross; most likely others were crucified with him; and that his crucifixion occurred where there were many passers-by (Mark 15:29); these all fit the historical record of Roman crucifixion practice. According to Mark's own narrative Jesus was abandoned by his disciples and his family. His only followers to witness the event were some women "looking on from a distance" (15:40). There was no one in close attendance who could give Mark such details as to what the passers-by said, Jesus' last words, what those crucified with him said, or what the centurion said. Those details are Markan creations used to tie Jesus to Old Testament prophesies.

To justify Mark's burial story we have to work backwards. Mark needed a tomb to be empty on Easter morning. As previously noted, the Romans rarely gave permission for anyone to claim a crucified body for burial. Even if Jesus' family had been around, as peasants they would have no influence to petition for the body. Mark gets around that issue by substituting Joseph of Arimathea, a "respected member of the council" (15:43), that is, Sanhedrin, for family. And he equivocates on the legalism of Deuteronomy

---

Barrabas was in jail for murder "during the insurrection," thus alluding to some sort of recent rebellious activity. Either way, allowing burial seems to be the exception rather than the rule.

27. Crossan, *Jesus: A Revolutionary*, 125–27; Ehrman, *How Jesus*, 160–61.

21:23—Jesus' crucifixion, after all, could not be considered as being for a crime—by substituting the approaching Sabbath as a reason to claim the body (15:42–43). To think that the Romans, ever contemptuous of Jewish sensitivities and religious customs, would have agreed to relinquishing Jesus' body is incompatible with historic Roman custom. As for Joseph of Arimathea, Mark contradicts himself. At 14:55 he tells us that the "whole council [was] looking for testimony against Jesus to put him to death," and at 15:1 he tells us that the "elders, scribes, and whole council" consulted, then had Jesus bound and sent him to Pilate. Why did Joseph, a member of the council who colluded in condemning Jesus to death in the morning, have a change of heart by afternoon, and suddenly claim Jesus' body for burial?[28] Because Mark needed a tomb to be empty on Easter morning to advance his Christology.

Mark's Passion Narrative, indeed of all four Passion Narratives, fall into a genre[29] of long use in Jewish texts—that of the suffering servant, or suffering Righteous One. This genre makes strong use of motifs from Psalms 22 and 69, and there is some evidence that the motif was present in the early church, as reflected in Romans 15:3.[30] Regardless of historical liberties taken, the underlying theme is that of the Righteous One, the payoff for some divine transgression, exalted after suffering at the hands of his enemies. We have noted in chapter 5 that this motif is well established in Psalms, especially Psalm 22, in the Wisdom of Solomon, and Maccabees. It can also be found in Susanna and other Jewish writings.[31]

Mark had to be creative with his Passion Narrative to justify the shamefulness of the crucifixion. Such justification was necessary to further his goal of proving Jesus was the Christ, the divine Messiah, the anointed of God. Mark's narrative places Jesus' humiliating fate within a schema his audience could understand. The discrepancies within his Gospel makes historical accuracy doubtful; but then, historical accuracy was not Mark's goal. The Passion Narrative does, however, contain the essence of the Christian foundational kerygma that Mark and the primitive church needed to

---

28 In all four Gospels it was the Jewish leaders who demanded Jesus be executed. In Acts 13:27–29 Paul states that it was the same leaders who demanded Jesus be executed also asked for the body to give it a proper burial. Opposing groups of Jewish leaders, or conflicting stories due to creative license? And what about the other two Jewish rebels crucified with Jesus, buried or not? If not, why?

29. Nickelsburg, "The Genre," 153–184, offers a detailed analysis of the genre.

30. Marshall, "The Death," 14.

31. Nickelsburg, *The Genre,* 154. *Susanna* is Chapter 13 of the Book of Daniel. It is included in the Septuagint and the Roman and Greek Orthodox Canon but not the Protestant Canon.

validate. Since Mark was writing during a most dangerous time for the Christian community in Rome, he had to be cautious. With the high priest's reaction, rending his clothes and attestation of blasphemy, and the council's conclusion that Jesus deserved to die, and by inserting the intercalations of Peter's denial, and the Barabbas anecdote, Mark skillfully deflects his audience's attention away from Roman involvement in the crucifixion. No matter how many twists and turns Mark takes, he still had to explain the fact that Jesus was crucified as a rebel by the Romans in accordance with Roman law and according to their routine brutal retribution for any threat to their authority. The titulus on Jesus' cross, "The King of the Jews" (15:26), proclaims justification for crucifixion but gives us no clue as to how the charge originated. It didn't really matter. It was not Roman but Jewish demands to "Crucify him!" (15:13–14) that will echo loud and long in the minds of Mark's first audience, and down through the centuries.

9

Mark's Theology

The beginning of the good news of Jesus Christ, the Son of God.

—MARK 1:1

MARK'S BRIEF INCIPIT NOT only opens his Gospel but also lays out his theological position—Jesus is the Messiah and the Son of God. Mark's main purpose in writing was to prove that Jesus of Nazareth, an apocalyptic prophet, executed by the Romans as a rebel, was the Messiah. Consequently, we are left asking two important questions. First, "Why, after nearly forty years, did Mark have to prove Jesus was the Christ and the Son of God?" and second, "What does his Gospel tell us about the *Sitz im Lieben* of the early church that prompted Mark to write that particular narrative in that particular form at that particular time?" The answers to those questions reflect the numerous conflicts and events that, in Mark's eyes, beset the primitive church.

Mark reached a decisive moment in his narrative with the burial of Jesus. His audience must have wondered why he introduced them to this purveyor of miracles and prophet of God's coming kingdom only to leave them with that miracle worker's lifeless body laid to rest in a stone tomb. What did it all mean? Mark attempts to give his audience a meaningful answer to that question with the last two significant parts of his Gospel: the empty-tomb story and the ending. While these two elements close his

Gospel, they open his theology. His unique empty-tomb story, in particular, is important to understanding his theology.[1] Mark wants his audience to understand the hope that Jesus' death brought to them. He starts this process by reaching back to pagan tradition while simultaneously preparing his audience for the impending apocalyptic future—the Parousia, the approaching kingdom of God.

THE EMPTY TOMB

Why an empty tomb? More specifically, why *only* an empty tomb? Mark's simple account of the empty tomb has opened the door to two thousand years of speculation. While all the other New Testament post-Markan accounts—Matthew, Luke, John, and Acts, albeit in differing detail—give us appearance stories to affirm Jesus had risen, bodily and spiritually, Mark gives us only an empty tomb and the word of a mystical young man to imply Jesus had been raised. What did Mark know, or not know, that persuaded him only to allude to the resurrection of his Messiah?

Whether or not the story of the empty tomb was part of the pre-Markan tradition is a matter of conjecture.[2] Certainly Mark gives us the first formal account of it. Paul may or may not have known of this account, but he never mentions it; his kerygmatic declaration in 1 Corinthians 15:3–5 states only that Jesus was resurrected, with no mention of an empty tomb. When the young man at the tomb says Jesus was "raised" (Mark 16:6) does he (Mark) mean a full-bodied, walking, talking, tangible resurrection, as later Evangelists portrayed it and as the modern Christian profession of faith proclaims it? Not necessarily. What did Mark have in mind? Neill Q. Hamilton thinks Mark gives us a clue in 12:24–25, when Jesus tells the Sadducees (who did not believe in resurrection) that after death one is like an "angel in heaven," which would not require a resurrected body.[3]

The idea of bodily resurrection of the dead had its origin in the Maccabean period.[4] It is first mentioned in the Bible in Daniel 12:2[5] but it is more succinctly referenced in 2 Maccabees 12:43–45, where Judas Maccabeus takes up a collection for his fallen troops who had worn forbidden pagan tokens into battle:

1. Hamilton, "Resurrection Tradition," 418.

2. Dibelius *From Tradition*, 181 does not think it was. MacGregor, "The Ending," 2, thinks it was.

3. Hamilton, "Resurrection Tradition," 418.

4. Cadbury, "Intimations," 3.

5. Koterski, *Daniel*, 126.

He also took up a collection, man by man, to the amount of two thousand drachmas of silver, and sent it to Hierosolyma [Jerusalem] to provide for a sin offering. In doing this he acted very well and honorably, taking account of the resurrection. For if he were not expecting that those who had fallen would rise again, it would have been superfluous and foolish to pray for the dead. But if he was looking to the splendid reward that is laid up for those who fall asleep in godliness, it was a holy and pious thought. Therefore he made atonement for the dead so that they may be delivered from their sin.

Resurrection was mystifying and controversial to Jews and Gentiles alike. Mark gives us a glimpse of its puzzling nature in 9:9–10: "As they were coming down the mountain [after the Transfiguration], he ordered them to tell no one about what they had seen until after the Son of Man had risen from the dead. So they kept the matter to themselves, *questioning what this rising from the dead could mean*" (italics added). According to Acts 4:1–3, "preaching the resurrection of the dead" was so annoying to the Jewish religious and political leaders that they had John and Peter arrested for it. Viewpoints of Jesus' "resurrection," the eventual linchpin of Christian dogma, varied within the primitive church.[6]

A plausible source for the empty-tomb theme may be found not in Christian but in Greco-Roman tradition. The empty-tomb story is, perhaps, not so much Mark's creation as it is his utilization of an already existing Hellenist and Roman afterlife belief that certain heroic individuals, such as Romulus, Castor, Pollux, and others were "taken up," that is, exalted, without a trace of bodily remains.[7] That Jesus' body was no longer in the tomb fulfills the Jewish, especially Maccabean, martyr motif of exaltation as a divine reward for the suffering servant (see chapter 5). In 2 Maccabees 7:9 the second brother declares with his dying breath: "You accursed wretch, you dismiss us from this present life, but the King of the universe will raise us up to an everlasting renewal of life, because we have died for his laws." When the fourth brother is near death, he says, "It is desirable that those who die at the hands of human beings should cherish the hope God gives of being raised again by him. But for you there will be no resurrection to life!" (2 Macc 7:14). And God tells Daniel that "you shall rise for your reward at the end of the days" (Dan 12:13).

Resurrection also meshes with the traditional Hellenistic hero-cult belief that an empty grave indicated that this hero as a "Son of God" was

6. Mack, *A Myth*, 101.
7. Miller, "Mark's Empty Tomb," 761–65.

removed from his grave by his divine father and, once raised, he spiritually existed and moved about within the confines of his lifetime geographical environs.[8] Mark plays to this cultural belief at 14:28 when Jesus tells the disciples that he will go to Galilee *after he is raised up*. He reinforces it in the empty-tomb story when the young man says to the women, "you are looking for Jesus of Nazareth" (in Galilee) and then tells them to tell the disciples that Jesus will meet them in Galilee (16:6–7). Not only does Mark capture the attention of his Roman/Hellenist audience with recognizable and acceptable cultural and religious motifs but simultaneously prepares believers for the near-at-hand Parousia.

If the empty-tomb story was not totally created by Mark he, at least, assimilated and embellished a pre-existing myth for his own use. While subsequent evangelists portray the risen Jesus as a walking, talking, tangible body, Mark does not portray the risen Jesus at all. Again, why? An empty tomb does not, as some conclude, take for granted resurrection. Henry Joel Cadbury offers essential background information on this issue:

> There were in fact other aspects of Judaism which both before and after the events of Easter the first Christians shared . . . One of these was quite different from any resurrection belief—the belief that in individual instances men had escaped death altogether. They were quite literally immortal—not in the sense that having died once they would live forever, but in the sense that they had not died and perhaps would not die. Instead of death and descent into Sheol they had experienced removal—ascension, assumption, rapture, are the names theology has used—and the instances first noted by the Jews and Christians, though differently described, are Enoch, Elijah, and probably Moses.[9]

Missing from Cadbury's list of terms for the various types of death-avoiding experiences, but widely recognized at that time, is *translation*.[10] Translation

---

8. Hamilton, "Resurrection Tradition," 418–19.

9. Cadbury, "Intimations," 6–7; see also Dunn, *Did the First Christians*, 84–89.

10. The idea of *translation* in Mark seems to have originated with the noted theologian Elias Bickermann in his 1924 article *Das leere Grab* (The Empty Tomb). Other prominent theologians have built their concurring or opposing theories on Bickermann's. Hamilton, "Resurrection Tradition," 415–21, and Weeden, *Mark: Traditions*, 106–11 generally agree with Bickermann. Bultmann, *History*, 290, and, especially, Bolt, "The Empty Tomb," 27–37, do not agree. My purpose here is not to promote one opinion over the other but rather to stay focused on Mark and his audience. Inferring what Mark was implying beyond what he wrote is "ingenious conjecture" leading to conflicting exegeses. Again, we must recognize our psychological schematic process of the need for filling in the unknown. In the historical religious and mythological culture of Mark's first-century semi-literate audience, translation would have made perfect sense.

means the taking up of the body which has not experienced death as we know it and without a trace of bodily remains, consequently leaving behind an empty tomb. According to Elias Bickermann, a resurrection would include post-mortem appearances, translation does not.[11] Various scholars argue that with the empty-tomb story Mark was *implying* a translation.[12] Scripture tells us that Moses, Enoch, and Elijah were translated. Moses' death was mysterious with no one knowing of a burial place (Deut 34:5–6); Elijah was taken up in a whirlwind (2 Kgs 2:11), and Enoch: "By faith Enoch was translated that he should not see death; and was not found, because God had translated him: for before his translation he had this testimony, that he pleased God" (Heb 11:5 KJV; also see Gen 5:24). These examples fit the Jewish religious tradition of God taking up his most pleasing servants. Mark's transfiguration story offered his audience an even stronger impression of the translation motif by placing Jesus between two venerated prophets, Moses and Elijah, both of whom were translated.[13] On two occasions (6:15, 8:28) Mark tells us there were many who thought Jesus was Elijah.

Jesus' being translated would have been well received within the afterlife schema of both Greeks and Jews. If tradition was rife with appearance stories, why would Mark avoid them in favor of an insinuation of translation? To explore this matter further requires a brief digression into an intriguing and crucial examination of the concept of Jesus as a *theios aner*.

THEIOS ANER

In first-century Hellenistic legend there existed the belief in the *theios aner* (pl. *theioi andres*)—divine man.[14] There are some who claim that the Gospels and Acts of the Apostles are themselves *aretalogies*, that is, stories about a *theios aner* from Nazareth named Jesus.[15] This belief was common among

11 In Bolt, "The Empty Tomb," 28.

12. Hamilton, "Resurrection Tradition," 416; Marxsen, *Mark the Evangelist*, 112–113; Weeden, *Mark: Traditions*, 106–111.

13. Bultmann, *History*, 259, suggests the transfiguration story was originally a resurrection story that Mark moved to its current place in his gospel. Placing Jesus between two revered translated individuals would have given Mark's Jewish audience a much different impression than it does to modern Christians.

14. The term and concept can be traced back to Plato's, *Meno* (99); Josephus identifies Jesus as a "wise man," a *sophos aner* (*Ant.* 18.3.3); Dibelius, *From Tradition*, 81 refers to them as the *thaumaturge*—miracle workers.

15. Smith, M., "Prolegomena," 176–78. While the Gospels are generally considered a unique literary genre, they are closest in form and theme to primitive aretalogies, stories of miracle workers with divine power, than to any other type of primitive literature (Smith, M., "Prolegomena," 196).

first-century Jewish Christians who recognized Jesus as a divine man.[16] No question there were eternal gods, such as Zeus and Yahweh, and, of course, there were mere mortals. Included among the mortals, however, was the occasional special individual upon whom God bestowed supernatural powers of wisdom, virtue, healing and other miracles. This person would be so virtuous and so favored by God that upon death he would be "taken up," that is, translated and granted immortality.

Belief in a *theios aner* was deeply embedded in Mark's world, and *theios aner* stories would have been quite familiar to his audience. The first-century concept of *theioi andres* was based on legends running far back in history. They were recognized in Egypt (Osiris), Greece (Heracles, Dionysus, Arisaeus), Rome (Aeneas, Romulus), and Israel (Moses, Elijah).[17] Apollonius of Tyana, who lived during Mark's time, was just such a figure.[18] Legend tells us that this man's life very much paralleled that of Jesus—a pre-birth announcement story, a celestial display at his birth, a peripatetic life of moral teaching and miracle work, a following of devoted supporters, and eventually claiming to be a Son of God and king of the Jews. That latter claim, not surprisingly, brought eventual arrest by the Roman authorities. Escaping from prison, Apollonius sought refuge in a sanctuary from where he departed this life unseen behind closed doors leaving behind no trace of his earthly body.[19] There are certain commonalities to be found in the *theioi andres*; for example, they all had a divine father and human mother, they all lived as mortals, during their life it was prophesized that upon their death they would be exalted, they were teachers, healers, doers of good, opposed evil, and they departed this world leaving no earthly remains but only a heavenly confirmation of their being taken up.[20] In Acts 2:22, Peter describes Jesus neither as the Messiah nor God incarnate, but as a *theios aner*: "Jesus of Nazareth, a man attested to you by God with deeds of power, wonders, and signs that God did through him among you, as you yourselves know."

Ironically, Mark himself contributed to his audience's perception of Jesus as a *theios aner*. Mark 3:7–10 is a prime example of the effect his miracle

---

16. Smith, M., "Prolegomena," 192.

17. Miller, "Mark's Empty Tomb," 761–67; Talbert, "The Concept of Immortals," 422–23, 425.

18. Talbert, "The Concept of Immortals," 425. Philostratus (ca. 170 to ca. 250 CE) presents an in-depth look at this unique individual in his *The Life of Apollonius of Tyana*.

19. Ehrman, *How Jesus Became God*, 13–24; Miller, "Mark's Empty Tomb," 765. Philostratus, *The Life*, 8.30, offers various stories about Apollonius's removal from this life.

20. Talbert, "The Concept of Immortals," 421–22.

work had on the crowd.[21] The emphasis on Jesus' miracle work in the first half of the Gospel combined with the suppression of his messiahship (the messianic secret) did not give the audience much reason to think differently. They would have experienced much less cognitive dissonance identifying Jesus as a *theios aner* than as a god. And therein lie a challenge, motive, and opportunity for Mark, which will be addressed shortly.

Numerous scholars recognize and address the Markan *theios aner* issue to a greater or lesser extent. Neil Hamilton and Theodore J. Weeden each, in particular, offer a thorough analyses of the meaning of Mark's empty-tomb story within the *theios aner* paradigm.[22] Mark's Hellenist/Roman audience would have easily made the connection between the centurion's proclamation of Jesus as Son of God (15:39) made shortly before the empty-grave story at 16:5–7—the body being taken up was indication of the individual being a *theios aner*.[23] Weeden and Hamilton agree that Mark's empty-grave story is a translation story meant to deal with a *Sitz im Leben* within the church marked by internal disagreement that threatened church unity.[24] Weeden presents a convincing argument that Mark's Gospel is an apologetic countering a growing *theios aner* heresy within the church.[25] In other words, the *Sitz im Leben* within the church was such that there were two competing groups: those who viewed Jesus as a *theios aner,* which was in opposition to those who followed Mark's portrayal of Jesus as suffering-servant Messiah. The suffering servant position was a *theologia crucis* (theology of the cross), the belief that Jesus' messiahship was to be found not in "wondrous works" but solely in his suffering servitude and death on the cross: "If any want to become my followers, let them deny themselves and take up their cross and follow me" (Mark 8:34). This was the root of Jesus' confrontation with Peter at Caesarea Philippi, when Peter rebuked Jesus for foretelling his rejection, suffering, and execution (Mark 8:27–33). Peter could not move beyond his human *theios aner* schema of the Messiah, he could not grasp that Jesus embodied the divine suffering-servant Messiah of the *theologia crucis*.[26]

After Caesarea Philippi, Mark focused less on miracle signs and more on the *theologia crucis* theme as he builds toward the climax in the crucifixion. By then, however, it may have been too late to change the schema of

---

21. Mark is not alone in this regard. John's "Signs Source" Gospel follows suit. See John 20:30–31, 21:25.

22. Hamilton, "Resurrection Tradition," 415–21; Weeden, "The Heresy," 148–150; Weeden, *Mark: Traditions,* 64, 106–107.

23. Hamilton, "Resurrection Tradition," 419.

24. Weeden, *Mark: Traditions,* 64, 106–7.

25. Weeden, "The Heresy," 148–150.

26. Weeden, "The Heresy," 148–150.

an audience that had come to know Jesus more as a *theios aner* than as the suffering-servant Messiah. After Caesarea Philippi even the disciples had no better comprehension of Jesus' true identity than they did before.[27] This is evident when Peter rebukes Jesus' *theologia crucis* prophecy. Why would Mark purposefully characterize the disciples as uncomprehending fools? Because he needed them to symbolize his *theios aner* opposition, that is, those who did not grasp the suffering-servant crucified Son of God, Jesus, as the true Messiah. From this perspective Mark's entire Gospel is an anti-*theios aner* argument.[28]

The growing *theios aner* heresy was fueled by the fact that Jesus was not the only "holy man" working the Palestinian theater. Messianic prophets were common in Palestine before, during, and after Jesus' life;[29] for example, Simon Magus, Apollonius of Tyana, and Bar-Jesus (Elymas) mentioned in Acts 13:6–8. Mark, no doubt familiar with such persons, alludes to them in Jesus' prophecy that, "Many will come in my name, and say 'I am he!'" (13:6) and "False messiahs and false prophets will appear and produce signs and omens to lead astray, if possible, the elect" (13:22). He was also aware of the allure such celebrated figures held for primitive Christians. Considering the ambiguity of Jesus' identity as a sub-theme in Mark's Gospel, when Jesus asks, "Who do people say that I am?" (8:27), Mark could well have been driving home his anti-*theios aner* argument by emphasizing Jesus' true identity with Peter's exclamation: "You are the Messiah" (8:30).

THE ENDING

The ending of Mark is, perhaps, the most controversial feature of his Gospel. The earliest extant renditions of the Gospel end at 16:8: "So they [the women] went out and fled from the tomb, for terror and amazement had seized them; and they said nothing to anyone, for they were afraid." Some scholars, Stein being one, contend that Mark wrote more after 16:8,[30] while

---

27. Wrede, *The Messianic Secret*, 116; Weeden, *Mark: Traditions*, 65, 148–49; Vaage, "Another Home," 745.

28. Weeden, *Mark: Traditions*, 147. Weeden, "The Heresy," 155–156; Vaage, "Another Home," 745. Stein, *Studying*, 264, disagrees that Mark was motivated by anti-*theios aner* concerns.

29. Horsley, "Popular Messianic Movements," 472; Smith, M., "Prolegomena," 180.

30. Stein, "The Ending," 92–97. While Stein agrees that 16:9–20 was written later by other redactors who were not satisfied with a 16:8 ending, he contends what Mark actually wrote, or intended to write, beyond 16:8 is lost to us. Regardless, what modern gospels have after 16:8 was not written by Mark.

others posit an even earlier end to the Gospel.[31] The earliest manuscripts, for example, the Codex Vaticanus and Codex Sinaiticus (both ca. 4th century CE), do not include any verses after 16:8.[32] Now, did Mark actually end his narrative with 16:8 or did he have a longer ending? That question is the nexus of a controversy that is much too complex to go into here. Based on the most widely-accepted conclusion among scholars, we will recognize 16:8 as the ending of Mark's Gospel.[33] This is a supportable conclusion given the earliest written sources end at 16:8. It is commonly accepted that verses 9 through 20 in our modern Bibles were added much later by other redactors who, one may justifiably assume, saw the lack of appearance episodes as so problematic that they added them to bring Mark into compliance with the Gospels that followed his. One clue in support of this conclusion is that verses 16:9–14 directly contradict 16:7. That fact raises an important point because how one interprets Mark's ending may influence how one perceives his theology.

With 16:8 as the Gospel's original Markan ending, then one of the following conclusions must be valid: 1) Mark did not know of any post-resurrection appearances; 2) the appearances were so well known that he felt no need to discuss them; therefore he purposefully left them out, 3) appearance stories would have contradicted his translation motif and therefore he again purposefully left them out, or 4) there were none to report. Paul tells us that Jesus first appeared to Peter (1 Cor 15:5), which contradicts Matthew (28:9), Luke (24:13–35), John (20:16), and Acts (1:3). In Acts 2:24 Peter attests to the resurrection but says nothing about a first post-resurrection encounter with Jesus. It is inconceivable that Peter would not have proudly informed Mark, presumably his close companion and interpreter, of such an event. For his part, Mark would have certainly used such a report from Peter (or anyone) as further proof to convince his audience that a resurrected Jesus was the Son of God and Messiah. If the first Christian audience knew of these appearances Mark surely would have written about them not only to confirm the validity of his story but also to underscore an essential theme of his Gospel. Mark, however, does not include any appearance stories despite their being part of tradition and alluded to in the kerygma. And the message from the young man at the tomb that Jesus would meet the disciples in Galilee,[34] along with no other report of a post-resurrection appearance,

31. Harris, "On the Alternative Ending," 96.

32. Henderson, "Discipleship," 109: Stein, "The Ending," 81.

33. Henderson, "Discipleship," 108; Ortlund, "Rising Language," 29.

34. Contrary to Mark 16:7 and Matthew 28:10 where Jesus directs the apostles to go and meet him in Galilee, Acts 1:4 declares "he ordered them not to leave Jerusalem."

puts Mark directly at odds with reports of Jesus' appearances in Acts and the other Gospels. Perhaps Mark created a scenario (Jesus being translated) that precluded post-resurrection appearances. The fact that the women, seized with terror and amazement "said nothing to anyone, for they were afraid" might explain why Mark had no post-resurrection appearances to relate—the disciples, never having gotten the message, did not return to Galilee as the man at the tomb instructed.

And yet we must acknowledge that subsequent appearance stories were based on something, be it reality, wishful thinking turned to fact, hallucinations, myth, or, although unverified, they had become "a solid piece of tradition [the Evangelists] were bound to respect."[35] While Hamilton and Weeden agree that the empty tomb story is one of translation they differ on what that means.[36] Whereas Hamilton sees it as an anti-resurrection story,[37] Weeden concludes that it is an anti-appearance story.[38] If translation calls for the empty tomb without a subsequent appearance, how then do we justify that with all of Mark's references to resurrection that does require an appearance? It is conceivable that "resurrected" is the language of tradition and Mark could hardly go against tradition; after all, he had written that Jesus prophesized his resurrection. It was also affixed in the confession in 1 Corinthians 15:3–5. Mark obfuscates the situation by writing *of* resurrection but not affirming it with appearance stories. His written words often read "resurrection" but his evidence—the empty tomb, no appearances, the transfiguration—implies "translation." This line of Markan empty-tomb interpretation demands a conceptual differentiation between resurrection and translation that is difficult to conceptualize today in any manner that approximates that of Mark's first-century audience.

What other reason might Mark have had for purposefully leaving appearance stories out of his narrative? Perhaps it was because the Parousia was more important to Mark than transient appearances. Cadbury reminds us that, "The expectation of living on until the *Parousia* may be the real reason why the Gospels say so little of resurrection."[39] Hamilton and Weeden both put forward the idea that in Mark's mind a resurrected Jesus was a distraction from the coming of the Son of Man in the Parousia.[40]

35. Dodd, *The Founder*, 167.

36. Hamilton and Weeden draw their conclusions from an array of other sources as well as their own research. Since it is far beyond the limits of this study to include them all, what is presented here is a summation of that cumulative work.

37. Hamilton, "Resurrection Tradition," 420.

38. Weeden, *Mark: Traditions,*108.

39. Cadbury, "Intimations," 25–26.

40. Hamilton, "Resurrection Tradition," 420; Weeden, *Mark: Traditions,*107.

The *immediate* physical re-appearance of Jesus was not essential to Mark's goal of affirming the fulfillment of Jesus' prophecies that the Son of Man would return to establish the kingdom of God. We know the concept of resurrection was controversial in first-century Judaism. Where the concept of resurrection did exist, it was understood to mean a *generalized* occurrence at the end time rather than a singular event.[41] The fact that Jesus had promised it would happen in their lifetime had to mean that he was coming soon—the Parousia had to be near because it seemed that the end time was near. In 13:29 Mark tells us: "So also, when you see these things taking place, you know that he [the Son of Man] is near, at the very gates." It is widely accepted that chapter 13 is a *vaticinum ex eventu* (see chapter 7) Mark created to validate the approaching end-time and Parousia. The end-time signs Jesus enumerates, events Mark had already witnessed then wrote as prophecy, included war, nation (Judea) rising against nation (Rome), massive earthquakes, believers being persecuted because of Jesus, people forced to flee to the hills, the *desolating sacrilege*, the destruction of the Temple, Palestine subjugated, the "pillars of the church" dead or in flight, the Jerusalem church eliminated, a growing *theios aner* challenge dividing the community, and conspiracy and betrayal infecting the church in Rome. These were undeniable signs of the end times and the impending arrival of God's kingdom. Mark's apocalyptic message was so essential that he impresses it upon his audience very early in his Gospel through Jesus' proclamation: "The time is fulfilled, and the kingdom of God has come near" (1:18). Mark wanted his Christian brothers and sisters to be ready and qualified for admission to God's kingdom. A church battling persecution from without and dissent from within was far from ready.

Most troubling of all, perhaps, was the fact that Jesus had not yet returned as he promised—and time was running out. The human Jesus was gone, and the divine Jesus had not returned as promised. The audience Mark was addressing was one generation removed from the historical Jesus and his apostles. The reality of their world was not miracles but persecution, destruction, and unfulfilled promises. If the already-resurrected Son of God had appeared before, why had he not returned as he promised?[42] Where was this self-proclaimed Son of Man and his new kingdom? As Mark surveyed all those events that pointed to the end of his world, the most anguishing must have been the fact the believers were losing faith in what he perceived

---

41. Miller, "Mark's Empty Tomb," 767.

42. This further validates the translation-rather-than-resurrection theory. Translation holds out the promise of a future return. Resurrection means the subject is already here. If Jesus had already returned then why had the Parousia not started?

to be the truth of Jesus.[43] We can see Mark's growing anxiety to inform his church, his audience, and the world of this truth in 13:10: "And the good news [the gospel] must first be proclaimed to all nations."[44] In chapter 13 Jesus says he will not return until all those signs of the end of time take place. Surely, the destruction of Jerusalem and the Temple were signs that the end was near; therefore, the Parousia must be near. A young Mark may not have viewed those calamitous events in the same ominous context as did the aging Mark. But as he grew older, time grew more precious. For Mark the end time and the return of Jesus the Son of Man had to be coming together in his here-and-now. Jesus had promised it would.

The ending of Mark's Gospel is certainly one of its more frustrating features. While there is strong evidence to support the translation position, Mark gives us just enough to keep the resurrection motif alive—except for appearance stories. For Christians to even consider the resurrection in any manner other than what has been embedded in their orthodox schema is almost unthinkable—unbearable to some, heretical to many. Nonetheless. the resurrection schema is not supported by Mark's Gospel. His narrative is about the suffering-servant who brought God's message only to be met with contempt and execution. It is a call to suffering discipleship that went unheeded. If the traditional resurrection with appearances was essential to Mark's message he would have written accordingly, but he did not, and we are left to search for meaning in what he did write, not in what we think he meant.[45]

Whether one accepts the *theios aner* and translation motif or not, it does provide answers to an interrogatory thread running through this study: *Why this Gospel, in this form, at this time?* Form follows function. Within the first eighteen verses of his narrative Mark tells us that what follows is 1) the good news of Jesus the Son of God, 2) the Messiah, and 3) that the kingdom of God is at hand. Proving those claims is the Gospel's function. The remainder of his narrative is the form that he chose to support those claims. Therein lies Mark's challenge, his motive, and his opportunity.

The only objective and logical conclusion to be drawn from what we know of the specifics of Roman crucifixion practices, Roman contempt for

43. Weeden, "The Heresy," 155.

44. If the resurrection and subsequent appearances were essential to the overall messianic good news, then this verse conflicts with 16:8. The failure of the women to tell anyone about the empty tomb and Jesus' message to meet him in Galilee essentially stopped or hindered the spread of the "good news." Could this be Mark's motive for writing?

45 See Crossan, *Jesus: A Revolutionary*, 160–61, for an entirely different resurrection schema.

Jewish religious customs and concerns, Pilate's excessive brutality, together with the contradictions in Mark's Gospel noted in the last chapter, is that the burial story and, by consequence, the empty-tomb story are not historical facts but improvised literary devices Mark used to tie up loose fragments of his narrative as well as advance his theology, the theology of suffering discipleship. They were especially needed to fulfill Jesus' prophetic allusion to the return of "the Son of Man . . . coming with the clouds of heaven" (14:62), that is, the Parousia, and to prepare his audience for that event. Faithful commitment to those claims was paramount for salvation through the Parousia—chronological accuracy, literalness, and historical correctness were not. The timing was necessitated by cultural political, and military events; conflict within the Christian communities, and the rising *theios aner* heresy within the church as well as the conviction that the Parousia was imminent. The delay in the arrival of the Parousia against a world seeming to be on the doorstep of the end-time lends an apprehensive, almost desperate, pleading to the end of Mark's Gospel.[46]

Hamilton and Weeden both agree that a resurrection story would have been a distraction that would take attention away from the nearing Parousia.[47] A resurrected Jesus, co-mingling with mortals, would have been confusing. If Jesus was already here, among us, why would he go away only soon to return again? Mark had to show that Jesus was the true Messiah and not a *theios aner*. Only through him could believers gain access to the fast-approaching kingdom of God. The destruction of Judea and the Temple was all the proof Mark needed to assure himself that the end time was near at hand. The Parousia was rapidly approaching and Christians had to know how to please God in order to gain admission into the rapidly-approaching Kingdom. With the collapse of the physical Temple in Jerusalem there arose the need for a new "Temple" that would transcend human destruction.

46. Marxsen, *Mark the Evangelist*, 92.

47. Hamilton, "Resurrection Tradition," 420; Weeden, *Mark: Traditions*, 107–09.

10

Transcendence Of Mark

No language, then, is sufficient to express the origin, the dignity, even the substance and nature of Christ.

—EUSEBIUS, *EH*

WHAT ARE WE TO make of the Gospel according to Mark? Mark was a captive of his time; as was his audience. So, too, was this Jesus-event and Mark's written account about that event. Mark fails in many respects to give a coherent, logical, historic accounting of Jesus' life, primarily because there were so few coherent logical facts about Jesus available to him. Mark's Gospel must be seen as a semi-factual attempt to present a story that is just beyond human ability to fully comprehend. The only way to present a rational story to his audience was for Mark to combine the various pre-existing Jesus stories with familiar Hellenist and Jewish cultural and religious motifs. For both Mark and his first audience those motifs formed the lens through which they viewed the world and filled the gaps needed to make whole the fragments of the Jesus story.

Imagine, for a moment, how different this Jesus would be with only the Gospel of Mark, that is, without the Gospels of Matthew, Luke, or John. There would be no nativity story, no lineage back to David, no virgin birth, no post-resurrection. In fact, Mark might have been quite perplexed by

Matthew's genealogy and nativity story, and by the God incarnate of John's Gospel. Jesus' divinity grew with each successive Gospel and augmented by the writings of the early church fathers. An objective reading of Mark, that is, a reading detached from two thousand years of religious bias and obfuscation, would give us a much simpler Jesus. Mark's Jesus was misunderstood by his family, the general population, and even by his closest followers. When Peter claims him to be the Messiah it is not clear that he means a materialistic, secular Messiah as defined by longstanding Jewish tradition, or a divine Messiah; the latter would require a schema change of what Messiah meant (see John 12:35). Jesus represented a change in the relationship between God and humanity. To the political and religious authorities that change came as a threat they had to deal with in the extreme (Mark 3:6). They understood all too well that everything Jesus did—his words, teaching, deeds, behavior, criticisms—was a direct challenge not only to their existing laws and traditions, both secular and religious, but also, and especially, to their authority. Jesus fit the mold of a rebel, and they dealt with him accordingly. Jesus was an agitator agitating for a change of how we live and relate to God. The challenge for Mark was to reframe the known, to reinterpret the misunderstandings about this lawfully executed criminal into a rational story of hope and salvation. He does this by attempting to braid together many of the disparate pre-existing Jesus stories in order to create an account of Jesus' life that would rationally reframe the meaning of Messiah in an effort to prepare the believers for Jesus' imminent return in the Parousia.

For the first few decades after the crucifixion, the primitive church was at odds over both the divinity and messianic nature of Jesus. The destruction of the Jerusalem church created a significant vacuum in the primitive church body, a vacuum that was quickly filled by the next most powerful element within the church—the Hellenistic Christ cult. It was within that cult that Jesus' divine messianic manifestation was generated and flourished. Of this transition Dibelius informs us that there was a "general development of primitive Christianity which passes from a historical person to his formal worship and finally to the cosmic mythological Christ of Gnosis, and to ecclesiastical Christology."[1] Once Jesus is cast as "Christ," the Messiah, his life and works could offer hope to a nation oppressed and salvation to a world in need of, although not always receptive to, a new covenant with God.

The structure of Mark's narrative follows the traditional Greek literary form, especially the Greek tragic drama motif most familiar in his culture. That his story had significant aretalogical overtones lent weight to the fact that his main character was no ordinary human but someone extraordinary.

---

1. Dibelius, *From Tradition*, 288.

His narrative is a variation on a theme, that of the suffering servant who gives his life to appease an irritated God; a theme that stretches back to ancient Greece. With the martyr's sacrifice the nation is spared divine retribution and the martyr is rewarded with life everlasting. Mark made use of Greco-Roman-Judeo themes that were well-embedded in his first-century culture, themes his audience readily understood and comfortably accepted. His genius is that he blends all this together to create a story of hope of salvation; a story that transcends all the historical reality.

Mark leaves us with these conundrums: A baptism that does not reveal an incarnate God; multi-use of abstract titles; a hint at divinity that, given the cultural context of the first century, could mean something else; a heroic main character who seems to purposefully avoid identification; a group of loyal followers who never grasp the meaning of the event within which they were involved and who in the end abandon their leader; an empty-tomb event that held more meaning in pagan mythology than in a new religious revelation; no post-death appearances; and an abrupt ending that fails to bring his narrative to comfortable closure. But then, perhaps Mark did not want his audience to be comfortable. Whether he intended to or not, he leaves us seeking the risen Christ. Isn't that what the Jesus event was meant to do?

How are we, two thousand years removed, to understand a story distilled from a culture rife with the myths and magical thinking intrinsic to its reality; a story translated from an ancient language, into another ancient language, then translated and edited numerous times over not to provide historic facts but to promote faith in an event that transcends facts. Mark meant to convey a message of revelation from the essence of God using the only means available—human language—that most obdurate barrier standing between us and God. And yet, his narrative of this man, Jesus, this Christ, transcends human language Such transcendence in Mark's Gospel, as in faith itself, cannot be pinned down to historic facts and woefully inadequate expressions like "Father" and "Son" to explain the nature of the Creator or the relationship between Creator and the created. The depth and complexity of the message of revelation lie outside the capacity and structure of human language to be fully comprehended—thus Eusebius's declaration: "No language, then, is suffiecient to express the origin, the dignity, even the substance and nature of Christ" (*EH*, 1.2).

The Gospel according to Mark is a mystery not waiting to be solved but an ongoing challenge to be pursued. Intentional or not, the ending of Mark's Gospel challenges us to seek the risen Christ. Beyond the myths, the legends, and the creative insertions Mark leaves us standing before Jesus and asked to answer: "Who do you say I am?"

Bibliography

The Acts of Peter. In *The Apocryphal New Testament.* Translated by M.R. James. Oxford: Clarendon Press, 1924. http://www.earlychristianwritings.com/text/actspeter.html.

Aeschylus. "Prometheus Bound." In *Four Plays of Aeschylus.* Translated by Edmund Dodge Anderson Morshead. 1908. https://en.wikisource.org/wiki/Four_Plays_of_Aeschylus_(1908)_Morshead/Prometheus_Bound.

Aristotle. *The Poetics.* Translated by S.H. Butcher. 1902. http://www.denisdutton.com/aristotle_poetics.htm.

———. *Rhetoric.* Translated by John Henry Freese. 1924. https://en.wikisource.org/wiki/Rhetoric_(Freese)/Book_1.

———. *Nicomichean Ethics* In *Philosophic Classics, Vol. 1: Thales to Saint Thomas.* Edited by Walter Kaufmann, 480–519. Englewood Cliffs: Prentice Hall, 1961.

Augustine. "De consensus evangelistrarum." In *Nicene and Post-Nicene Fathers*, First Series, Vol. 6, edited by Philip Schaff. Buffalo: Christian Literature Publishing Co, 1888. https://www.newadvent.org/fathers/1602102.htm.

Aune, David E. "Prolegomena to the Study of Oral Tradition in the Hellenistic World." In *Jesus and the Oral Gospel Tradition*, edited by Henry Wansbrough, 59–106. New York: T & T Clark International, 1991.

Aslan, Reza. *Zealot: The Life and Times of Jesus of Nazareth.* New York: Random House, 2013.

Bakker, Hendrik Adrianus. "Beyond the Measure of Man: About the Mystery of Socratic Martyrdom." *Church History and Religious Culture* 9, 4 (2015): 391–407.

Beattie, D.R.G., and Philip R. Davies. "What does Hebrew Mean?" *Journal of Semitic Studies* LVI/I (Spring 2017): 1–83.

Beck, Aaron T. and David A. Clark. "Anxiety and Depression: An Information Processing Perspective." In *Anxiety Research*, 23–36. London: Harwood Academic, 1988.

Beck, Norman A. "The Last Supper as an Efficacious Symbolic Act." *Journal of Biblical Literature* 89, 2 (June 1970) 192–98.

Bickermann, Elias. "Das leere Grab [The Empty Tomb]." *Zeitschrift für die Neutestamentliche Wissenschaft und die Kunde der Älteren Kirche* 23, 2 (1924): 281–292.

Bilezikian, Gilbert G. *The Liberated Gospel: A Comparison of the Gospel of Mark and Greek Tragedy.* Eugene: Wipf & Stock, 1977.

Blackburn, Barry. "Deus et Homo: Jesus in the Gospels." *Stone-Campbell Journal* 4, 2 (Fall 2001): 187–204.

Bolt, Peter G. "Mark 16:1–8: 'The Empty Tomb of a Hero?'" *Tyndale Bulletin* 47, 1. (May 1996): 27–37.

Borges, Jorge Luis. "The Gospel According to Mark." In *Doctor Brodie's Report*. Translated by Norman Thomas Di Giovanni. New York: Bantam, 1973. https:// theteacherscrate.files.wordpress.com/2015/09/borges-jorge-luis-doctor-brodies-report-bantam-1973.pdf.

Bovon, François. "The Emergence of Christianity." *Annali di storia dell'esegesi* 24, 1 (2007): 13–29.

Brandon, S.G.F. *The Trial of Jesus of Nazareth*. New York: Dorset, 1968.

Bultmann, Rudolf. *History of the Synoptic Tradition*. Translated by John Marsh. New York: Harper & Row, 1963.

Cadbury, Henry Joel. "Between Jesus and the Gospels." *Harvard Theological Review* 16, 1 (January 1923): 81–92.

———. "Intimations of Immortality in the Thought of Jesus." *Harvard Theological Review* 53, 1 (January 1960): 1–26.

———. "Gospel Study and Our Image of Early Christianity." *Journal of Biblical Literature* 83, 2 (June 1964): 139–45.

Castor, George DeWitt. "The Relation of Mark to the Source Q." *Journal of Biblical Literature* 31, 2: 12 (1912): 82–91.

Chapman, David W. "Perceptions of Crucifixion Among Jews and Christians in the Ancient World." *Tyndale Bulletin* 51, 2 (2003): 313–16.

Clement. *Letter to the Corinthians (Clement)*. Translated by John Keith. https://www. newadvent.org/fathers/1010.htm.

Collins, Adela Yarbro. "Finding Meaning in the Death of Jesus." *The Journal of Religion* 78, 2 (April 1998): 175–96.

———. "Mark and His Readers: The Son of God Among Jews." *Harvard Theological Review* 92, 4 (1999): 393–408.

———. "Mark and His Readers: The Son of God Among Greeks and Romans." *Harvard Theological Review* 93, 2 (April 2000): 85–100.

———. "The Charge of Blasphemy in Mark 14:64." *Journal for the Study of the New Testament* 26, 4 (June 2004): 379–401.

Conzelmann, Hans. "History and Theology in the Passion Narratives of the Synoptic Gospels." *Interpretation* 24 (1970): 178–97.

Crossan, John Dominic. *Jesus: A Revolutionary Biography*. New York: HarperCollins, 1995.

Cullmann, Oscar. "Dissension Within the Early Church." *Union Seminary Quarterly Review* 22, 2 (1967): 83–92.

Dawsey, James. *Peter's Last Sermon: Identity and Discipleship in the Gospel of Mark*. Macon: Mercer, 2010

DeBoer, Willis P. "Saint Paul versus Saint Peter: A Tale of Two Missions." *Calvin Theological Journal* 32, 1 (1997): 164–68.

Deissmann, Adolf. *Light from the Ancient East*. 2nd ed. Translated by Lionel R. M. Strachan. New York: Hodder and Stoughton, 1911.

Dewey, Joanna. "The Gospel of Mark as an Oral/Aural Narrative: Implications for Preaching." *Currents in Theology and Mission* 44, 4 (2017): 7–10.

Dibelius, Martin. *From Tradition to Gospel.* Translated by Betram E. Woolf. New York: Charles Scribner's Sons, 1965.

Dixon, Edward P. "Descending Spirits and Descending Gods: A 'Greek' Interpretation of the 'Spirit's Descent as a Dove' in Mark 1:10." *Journal of Biblical Literature* 128, 4 (Winter 2009): 759–80.

Dodd, C.H. *The Founder of Christianity.* London: MacMillan, 1970.

Donahue, John R. *Are You the Christ? The Trial Narrative in the Gospel of Mark.* Missoula: Society of Biblical Literature, 1973.

Dunn, James D. G. *Did the First Christians Worship Jesus? The New Testament Evidence.* Louisville: WJK, 2010.

Eastman, David L. "Jealousy, Internal Strife, and the Deaths of Peter and Paul: A Reassessment of 1 *Clement.*" *Zeitschrift für antikes Christentum* 18, 1 (2014): 34–53.

Edwards, James R. "The Baptism of Jesus in the Gospel of Mark." *Journal of the Evangelical Theological Society* 34, 1 (March 1991): 43–57.

Ehrman, Bart D. *How Jesus Became God: The Exaltation of a Jewish Preacher from Galilee.* New York: HarperCollins, 2014.

Ellis, E. Earle. "The Making of Narratives in the Synoptic Gospels." In *Jesus and the Oral Gospel Tradition*, edited by Henry Wansbrough, 310–33. London: T & T Clark, 1991.

England, Stephen J. "The Tradition of the Life and Teachings of Jesus in the 'Kerygma.'" *Encounter* 21, 1 (Winter 1960): 81–92.

English, Schuyler E. "Was St. Peter Ever in Rome?" *Bibliotheca Sacra* 124, 496 (October 1967): 314–20.

Enslin, Morton S. "The Artistry of Mark." *Journal of Biblical Literature* 66, 4 D (1947): 385–99.

Euripides. "Iphigenia in Aulis." Text prepared by B. E. Turner. http://users.actrix.co.nz/b.turner/Iphigenia.pdf.

Eusebius Pamphilus. *The Ecclesiastical History of Eusebius Pamphilus.* Translated by Christian Fredrick Cruse. Grand Rapids: Baker, 1993.

Evans, Craig. "Jewish Burial Traditions and the Resurrection of Jesus." *Journal for the Study of the Historic Jesus* 3, 2 (2005): 233–45.

Gerhardsson, Birger. *Memory & Manuscript: Oral Tradition and Written Transmission in Rabbinic Judaism and Early Christianity.* Grand Rapids: Eerdmans, 1998.

Girard, Rene. *The Scapegoat.* Translated by Yvonne Freccero. Baltimore: Johns Hopkins University Press, 1986.

Gonzàlez, Justo L. *A History of Christian Thought: From the Beginnings to the Council of Chalcedon.* Vol. 1. Nashville: Abingdon, 1970.

Grobel, Kendrick. "Idiosyncracies of the Synoptists in Their Pericope-Introductions." *Journal of Biblical Literature* 59, 3 (1940): 405–10.

Guy, Harold. *The Origin of the Gospel of Mark.* New York: Harper and Brothers, 1955.

Hamilton, Neill Quinn. "Resurrection Tradition and the Composition of Mark." *Journal of Biblical Literature* 84, 4 D (1965): 415–21.

Harakas, Stanley S. "Must God Remain Greek?" *The Ecumenical Review* 43, 2 (April 1991) 194–99.

Harmon-Jones, Eddie. "A Cognitive Dissonance Theory Perspective on the Role of Emotion in the Maintenance and Change of Beliefs and Attitudes." In *Emotions and Beliefs: How Feelings Influence Thoughts,* edited by Nico H. Frijda et al, 185–211. Cambridge: Cambridge University Press, 2000.

Harris, James Rendel. "On the Alternative Ending of St. Mark's Gospel." *Journal of Biblical Literature* 12, 2 (1893): 96–103.

———. *Boanerges.* Cambridge: Cambridge University Press 1913. https://babel.hathitrust.org/cgi/pt?id=uc2.ark:/13960/t59c75s4q&view=1up&seq=216.

Hatina, Thomas R. "The Focus of Mark 13:24-27: The Parousia, or the Destruction of the Temple?" *Bulletin for Biblical Research* 6 (1996): 43–66.

Head, Peter M., and Peter J. Williams. "Q Review." *Tyndale Bulletin* 54, 1 (2003): 119–44.

Henderson, Suzanna Watts. "Discipleship After the Resurrection: Scribal Hermeneutics in the Longer Ending of Mark." *The Journal of Theological Studies* 63, 1 (April 2012): 106–24.

Homer. *Homeric Hymn.* Translated by Hugh G. Evelyn-White. Cambridge, MA: Loeb Classical Library, 1914. https://www.platonic-philosophy.org/files/Homeric%20Hymns.pdf.

———. *The Odyssey.* Translated by Robert Fagles. https://www.boyle.kyschools.us/UserFiles/88/The%20Odyssey.pdf.

Honey, T E Floyd. "Did Mark use Q?" *Journal of Biblical Literature,* 62, 4D (1943): 319–31.

Horsley, Richard A. "Popular Messianic Movements Around the Time of Jesus." *The Catholic Biblical Quarterly* 46, 3 (July 1984): 471–95.

Irenaeus, *Against Heresies.* Translated by Alexander Roberts and William Rambaut. 1885. https://www.newadvent.org/fathers/0103301.htm

Jewish Study Bible. Jewish Publication Society Tanakh translation. Edited by Adele Berlin and Marc Zvi Brettler. New York: Oxford University Press, 1999.

Josephus, Flavius. *The Jewish Antiquities.* Translated by William Whiston. https://en.wikisource.org/wiki/The_Antiquities_of_the_Jews.

——— . *The War of the Jews.* Translated by William Whiston. https://en.wikisource.org/wiki/The_War_of_the_Jews.

Justin Martyr, "1 Apology." In *Ante-Nicene Christian Library/The First Apology of Justin Martyr.* Translated by Marcus Dods. https://en.wikisource.org/wiki/Ante-Nicene_Christian_Library/The_First_Apology_of_Justin_Martyr.

Keck, Leander E. "Mark 3:7-12 and Mark's Christology." *Journal of Biblical Literature* 84, 4 D (1965): 341–48.

Kingsbury, Jack Dean. "The 'Divine Man' as the Key to Mark's Christology—The End of an Era?" *Interpretation* 35, 3 (July 1981): 243–57.

Kloppenborg, John S. "The Sayings Gospel Q and the Quest of the Historical Jesus." *Harvard Theological Review* 89, 4 (October 1996): 307–44.

Kloppenborg, John S. and Leif E. Vaage. "Early Christianity, Q and Jesus: The Sayings Gospel and Method in the Study of Christian Origins." *Semeia* 55 (1991): 1–14.

Koester, Helmut. "One Jesus and Four Primitive Gospels." *Harvard Theological Review* 61, 2 (April 1968): 203–47.

Kok, Michael J. "The Flawed Evangelist (John) Mark: A Neglected Clue to the Reception of Mark's Gospel in Luke-Acts?" *Neotestamentica* 46, 2 (2012): 244–259.

Koterski, Joseph W., SJS. "Daniel—God's Providential Plan for History." Lecture 27 in *Biblical Wisdom Literature,* disc 14, ch. 27, track 4. 18 compact discs. CD-ROM. The Great Courses. Chantilly: The Teaching Company, 2009.

Kraus, C. Norman. "The Early Church Encounters the Graeco-Roman World." *Mennonite Quarterly Review* 37, 4 O (1963): 251–78.

Lea, Thomas D. and David Alan Black. *The New Testament: Its Background and Message.* 2nd ed. Nashville: Broadman & Homan, 2003.

Liefeld, Walter L. "The Hellenistic 'Divine Man' and the Figure of Jesus in the Gospels." *Journal of the Evangelical Theological Society* 16, 4 (Fall 1973): 195–205.

Lipson, Marjorie Youmans. "The Influence of Religious Affiliation on Children's Memory for Text Information." *Reading Research Quarterly* 48, 4 (Summer 1983): 448–57.

Lührmann, Dieter. "The Gospel of Mark and the Sayings Source Q." *Journal of Biblical Literature* 108, 1 (Spring 1989): 51–71.

MacArthur, James. *Guidelines for a Happy Christian Life.* Nashville: Thomas Nelson, 2007.

MacDonald, Dennis. *The Homeric Epics and the Gospel of Mark.* New Haven: Yale University Press, 2000.

MacGregor, Kirk Robert. "The Ending of the Pre-Markan Passion Narrative." *Scriptura* 117, 1 (2018): 1–11.

Mack, Burton L. "The Innocent Transgressor: Jesus in Early Christian Myth and History." *Semeia* 33 (1985): 135–65.

———. "Q and the Gospel of Mark: Revising Christian Origins." *Semeia* 55 (1991): 15–39.

———. "Redescribing Christian Origins." *Method & Theory in the Study of Religion* 8, 3 (1996): 247–69.

———. *A Myth of Innocence: Mark and Christian Origins.* Minneapolis: Fortress, 2006.

Marshall, I. Howard. "The Death of Jesus in Recent New Testament Study." *Word & World* 3, 1 (Winter 1983): 12–21.

Marxsen, Willi. *Mark The Evangelist: Studies on the Redaction History of the Gospel.* Translated by James Boyce, et al. 2nd ed. Nashville: Abingdon, 1969.

McCrum, Robert, William Cran, and Robert MacNeil. *The Story of English.* New York: Penguin Books, 1992.

McKechnie, Paul. *The First Christian Centuries.* Downers Grove: Intervarsity, 2001.

Meier, John P. "The Historic Jesus and the Historic Herodians." *Journal of Biblical Literature* 119, 4 (Winter 2000): 740–46.

Miller, Richard C. "Mark's Empty Tomb and Other Translation Fables in Classical Antiquity." *Journal of Biblical Literature* 12, 4 (2010): 759–76.

Narvaez, Darcia, and Tonia Bock. "Moral Schema and Tacit Judgment, or How the Defining Issues Test is Supported by Cognitive Science." *Journal of Moral Education* 31, 3 (2002): 297–314.

Moriarity, W. "1 Clement's View of Ministerial Appointments in the Early Church." *Vigiliae Christianae* 66, 2 (2012): 115–138.

Nickelsburg, George W E. "The Genre and Function of the Markan Passion Narrative." *Harvard Theological Review* 73, 1–2 (January–April 1980): 153–184.

Ortlund, Dane. "Rising Language in Mark and the Dawning New Creation." *Criswell Theological Review* 13, 2 (Spring 2016): 27–45.

Osborne, Grant R. *The Hermeneutical Spiral: A Comprehensive Introduction to Biblical Interpretation.* 2nd ed. Downers Grove: Intervarsity, 2006.

Outler, Albert Cook. "The Gospel According to St. Mark." *Perkins Journal* 33, 4 (Summer 1980): 3–9.

Pearson, Birger A. "Christians and Jews in First-Century Alexandria." *Harvard Theological Review* 79, 1–3 (January–July 1986): 206–16.

Perrin, Norman. "The Creative Uses Of the Son of Man Traditions by Mark." *Union Seminary Quarterly Review* 23, 4 (Summer 1968): 357–65.

———. "The Son of Man in Ancient Judaism and Primitive Christianity: A Suggestion." *Biblical Research* 11 (1966): 17–28.

Philostratus. *Life of Apollonius of Tyana.* Translated by F.C. Conybear. https://www.livius.org/sources/content/philostratus-life-of-apollonius/philostratus-life-of-apollonius-8.26–31/#8.31.

Piper, Otto Alfred. "The Origin of The Gospel Pattern." *Journal of Biblical Literature* 78, 2 Je (1959): 115–124.

Plato. *Apology.* In *Philosophic Classics, Vol. 1: Thales to Saint Thomas.* Edited by Walter Kaufmann, 99–112. Englewood Cliffs: Prentice Hall, 1961.

———. *Meno.* In *Philosophic Classics, Vol. 1: Thales to Saint Thomas.* Edited by Walter Kaufmann, 118–45. Englewood Cliffs: Prentice Hall, 1961.

———. *Phaedrus.* In *Philosophic Classics, Vol. 1: Thales to Saint Thomas.* Edited by Walter Kaufmann, 201–53. Englewood Cliffs: Prentice Hall, 1961.

Reedy, William J. "About the Kerygma." *Religious Education* 57, 5 (September–October 1962): 349–55.

Rest, James. *Postconventional Moral Thinking: A neo-Kohlbergian Approach.* Mahwah: Lawrence Erlbaum, 1999.

Reynolds, John Mark. *When Athens Met Jerusalem: An Introduction to Classical and Christian Thought.* Downers Grove: IVP Academic, 2009.

Ricoeur, Paul. *The Symbolism of Evil.* Translated by Emerson Buchanan. Boston: Beacon, 1967.

Saint Jerome. *The New Jerome Biblical Commentary.* Edited by Raymond E. Brown et al. Upper Saddle River: Prentice Hall, 1990.

Simkovich, Malka Zeiger. "Greek Influence on the Composition of 2 Maccabees." *Journal for the Study of Judaism* 42 (2011): 293–310.

Smith, Morton. "Prolegomena to a Discussion of Aretalogies, Divine Men, the Gospels and Jesus." *Journal of Biblical Literature* 90, 2 (June 1971): 174–99.

Smith, Stephen. "A Divine Tragedy: Some Observations on the Dramatic Structure of Mark's Gospel." *Novum testamentum* 37, 3 (July 1995): 209–31.

Snape, Henry Currie. "Christian Origins in Rome, with Special Reference to Mark's Gospel." *Modern Churchman* 13, 3 (April 1970): 230–44.

———. "Peter and Paul in Rome." *Modern Churchman* 14, 2 (January 1971): 127–38.

Sophocles. "Antigone." In *The Tragedies of Sophocles.* Translated by Richard Claverhouse Jebb. 1917. https://en.wikisource.org/wiki/Tragedies_of_Sophocles_(Jebb_1917)/Antigone.

Stählin, Gustav. "On the Third Day: The Easter Traditions of the Primitive Church." Translated by Wayne P. Todd. *Interpretation* 10, 3 (1956): 282–99.

Stein, Robert H. "What is Redactiongeschiccte?" *Journal of Biblical Literature* 88, 1 (1969): 45–56.

———. "The Proper Method for Ascertaining a Markan Redaction History" *Novum Testamentum* 13, 3 (1971): 181–98.

———. "Is the Transfiguration (Mark. 9:2–8) a Misplaced Resurrection Account?" *Journal of Biblical Literature* 95, 1 (March 1976): 79–96.

———. *Studying the Synoptic Gospels: Origin and Interpretation.* 2nd ed. Grand Rapids: Baker Academic, 2001.

———. "Is Our Reading the Bible the Same as the Original Audience's Hearing It? A Case Study in the Gospel of Mark." *Journal of the Evangelical Theological Society* 46, 1 (2003): 63–78.

———. "The Ending of Mark." *Bulletin for Biblical Research* 18, 1 (2008) 79–98.

Suetonius, C. Tranquillus. *Lives of the Caesars, Claudius, XXV.* Translated by Alexander Thomson, M.D. 2016. https://www.gutenberg.org/files/6400/6400-h/6400-h.htm#link2H_4_0007.

Tacitus, Cornelius. *The Annals.* Translated by Alfred John Church and William Jackson Brodribb. 1876. https://en.wikisource.org/wiki/The_Annals_(Tacitus)/Book_15.

Talbert, Charles H. "The Concept of Immortals in Mediterranean Antiquity." *Journal of Biblical Literature* 94, 3 (September 1975): 419–36.

Talmon, Shemaryahu. "Oral tradition and Written Transmission, or the Heard and the Seen Word in Judaism of the Second Temple Period." In *Jesus and the Oral Gospel Tradition.* Edited by Henry Wansbrough, 121–58. London: T & T Clark, 1991.

Vaage, Leif E. "Another Home: Discipleship in Mark as Domestic Asceticism." *The Catholic Biblical Quarterly* 71, 4 (October 2009): 741–61.

Vassiliadis, Petros. "Beyond Theologia Crucis: Jesus of Nazareth From Q to John *via* Paul (or John as a Radical Reinterpretation of Jesus of Nazareth)." *Greek Orthodox Theological Review* 47 (2002): 1–4.

Walls, Andrew F. "Converts or Proselytes? The Crisis Over Conversion in the Early Church." *International Bulletin of Missionary Research* 28, 1 (January 2004): 2–6.

Wallis, Ian G. "Why Mark Wrote a Gospel: Taking Another Look." *Modern Believing* 57, 1 (2016): 47–56.

Wenham, John William. "Did Peter go to Rome in A.D. 42?" *Tyndale Bulletin* 23 (1972): 94–102.

Weeden, Theodore. "The Heresy that Necessitated Mark's Gospel." *Zeitschrift für die neutestamentliche Wissenschaft und die Kunde der älteren Kirche* 59, 3—4 (1968): 145–58.

———. *Mark: Traditions in Conflict.* Philadelphia: Fortress Press, 1971.

Williams, Sam K. *Jesus' Death as Saving Event: The Background and Origin of a Concept.* Missoula: Scholars Press for Harvard Theological Review, 1975.

Wrede, William. *The Messianic Secret.* Translated by J.C.G. Grieg. London: James Clarke, 1971.

Index

CPSIA information can be obtained
at www.ICGtesting.com
Printed in the USA
LVHW020324070921
697165LV00003B/47

9 781666 707960